How to Get Fired!

The New Employee's Guide to Perpetual Unemployment

Jeff Havens

5554 Shamrock Lane
Madison, WI 53711
Phone: (608) 663-4723
Fax: (608) 663-4724
www.jeffhavens.com

Ordering Information

Special discounts are available on quantity purchases by colleges, corporations, associations, and others.   For details, contact the Quantity Sales Department at the address above.

Printed in the United States of America.

ISBN-13: 978-0-9843022-0-8
ISBN-10: 0-9843022-0-4

Cover design by Adam Havens
Interior illustrations by Billy Phillips

Dedication

To all the lazy, incompetent, arrogant, uncooperative, self-absorbed, deceitful, gossip-mongering, intolerant, perpetually complaining people who get fired every year, without whom this book could not have been written.

How to Get Fired!

The New Employee's Guide to Perpetual Unemployment

Why You Need This Book

Welcome, and congratulations on either purchasing or stealing your very own copy of *How to Get Fired!* By choosing to open this book, you have made a conscious decision to avoid the soul-crushing existence that comes from having a full-time job. You've enjoyed your last six or twelve years in college – filled as I'm sure they have been with snowball fights, beer pong, drunken hookups, late-night Waffle House runs, and the occasional, accidental moment of formal learning – and you're in no hurry to trade your current carefree life for one filled with stress and responsibility.

More importantly, you've seen your parents wither away, their smiles fading and their hair slowly falling out as they slog day after day after day through the soupy muck of the working world. Remember when they used to laugh instead of weeping for no apparent reason? Remember how spry they used to be, how easily they could lift you onto their shoulders and twirl you around the yard? When was the last time that happened – ten, fifteen years ago? The daily grind caught up to them, and there was nothing you could do.

Or perhaps you have friends who've graduated before you, and you've watched them transform into people you never thought they'd be – sad, pathetic wretches forced to comb their hair every day and wear watches and who occasionally *choose* to go to bed before midnight in order to summon the strength they'll need to face another unspeakably productive day at the office. You've watched it happen, and I know you've sworn to yourself, in a moment of blinding clarity while others held your legs for a marathon keg stand: *That's not going to happen to me.* And so again, congratulations for finding this book.

In these pages you will acquire all the wisdom necessary to ensure that you never have to suffer the burden of stable employment for very long. Every piece of information in this book has been market-tested. Thousands of people – nay, *hundreds of thousands* – have used the techniques in this book to shortcut their way straight into the unemployment line. Most of what you'll read is not new. But until now no one had thought to compile this information. Imagine the countless workers forced to figure out how to get fired all on their own, stumbling blindly through the mazes until stubborn determination or dumb luck allowed them the sweet release you now seek for yourself. That's why I have taken it upon myself to write this book, to ensure that nobody has to struggle to get fired in the future, and it is the reason that I fully expect to see statues of myself erected in honor of me around the world before I die.

As you will already have noticed, this book assumes that you either have attended or are currently in college. However, you don't have to have gone to college to appreciate what this book has to offer. *How to Get Fired!* is intended for anybody new to the professional world, whether you're about to graduate from high school, trade school, college, or prison. In most cases, the ideal reader of this book is under 30. Those of you who are older or who have held stable jobs for the past several years will undoubtedly be familiar with most of the advice in this book, because you'll have seen some of your coworkers use these concepts to secure their own successful terminations. Of course you're welcome to read this book too – after all, it might give you some pleasure by reminding you of your former, fallen colleagues. But for those of you about to embark into the wide world of resumes, benefits, power lunches, conference calls, teambuilding seminars, and everything else in the depressing world of adulthood, this book is indispensable.

Now I know some of you think you don't need this book. You've paid attention to the current recession and its deleterious effect on our employment rate. You've seen wave after wave of outsourcing remove thousands of jobs from the manufacturing, textile, technology, and information systems sectors. You've seen the parking lot at your local movie theater full on weekday afternoons. And you're thinking to yourself, "I don't need to do anything to get fired; it's so easy right now I should be perfectly fine."

Don't allow yourself to be persuaded by such slippery logic. There are two reasons you'll need this book. The first is that those issues mentioned above – downsizing, outsourcing, recessions, etc. – are things you can't control. They just happen; they're part of the nature of a market economy. *How to Get Fired!* focuses on the things you *can* control, the things you yourself can do to assure that you are never employed for very long. I want to put the power in your hands so that you won't be beholden to the whims of impersonal market forces.

Why should it matter? It matters because of the second reason you'll need this book, which is this: someday the economy is going to get better. Someday the unemployment level will taper off, then fall back to so-called 'healthier' levels. Someday there might even be, dare I say it, an *excess* of available jobs. And if that terrible day ever comes, if we are ever unfortunate enough to have more jobs available than there are workers to fill them, it will be much, much harder to get fired than it is now. That's why you need *How to Get Fired!*, so that you'll know how to lose a job *in any economy*.

I also imagine that some of you are wondering what makes me qualified to write this book. That's a very good question for which I have a very good answer. To put it simply, I have been fired from more jobs than you are likely to ever have. Some of the best and not-so-best companies in America – from Google and Boeing to Enron and Steamy's Gentlemen's Club – have decided that I am not worth a paycheck. The longest job I've ever held lasted exactly 43 days, during which time my parents began to seriously worry that I might one day move out of the house. But true to form, it ended in spectacularly bad fashion, and I am still comfortably ensconced in my family's basement, feasting on box macaroni whenever I please and drowning in World of Warcraft megaquests. As of the writing of this preface, I have gone six days without a shower. I have achieved nirvana, my future acolyte, and I can guarantee that if you follow the lessons in this book you will find the same glory I have.

So, without further adieu, let's highlight the main points we'll be covering.

The following is the result of hours of Internet[1] research coupled with conversations with hundreds of business owners from dozens of industries across the United States. Together, they've helped me compile a Top Ten List of the reasons,

---

[1] The Internet itself is a fantastic tool to help get yourself fired, which I have used on several occasions with remarkable success. We'll cover how it can help you in more detail in the awesomely titled chapter *The Internet*.

excluding layoffs and recession-based cutbacks, that most commonly lead to employees getting fired.

Top Ten Reasons People Get Fired

(excluding layoffs, recessions, depressions, natural disasters, outsourcing, downsizing, or setting your building on fire)

Lying on your resume

Unreliable work and behaviors

Inability to do assigned job tasks

Performing tasks slowly,
    with numberous errors[2]

High absenteeism

Conducting personal business
    at work

Drug and/or alcohol abuse

Dishonesty on the job

Refusing to follow
    directions and orders

Inability to get along with others

These are not listed in order of popularity; lying on your resume is not necessarily the most effective way to get fired. Rather, I have organized these behaviors in order to better discuss the major themes of getting fired – or as I like to

---

[2] Anyone catch the misspelled word in the one about making mistakes? I am hilarious.

call them, the Four Pillars of Poverty. The Pillars are, respectively:

1) Fake your resume
2) Establish your incompetence
3) Destroy your work ethic
4) Alienate your coworkers[3]

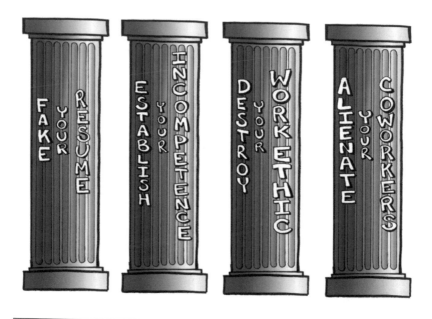

---

[3] For those of you who have heard the lecture associated with this book, you will know that this section was originally titled "Being an *******." However, I decided to write this book without cursing, and none of the ******* substitutes that I thought of – Jerkwad, Meanie, Doodyhead, Dingleberry, etc. – had the pure, evocative power of the ******* they were designed to replace. So I gave up and went with a safer, albeit more pedestrian, title. My apologies to the obscure-indie-rock-loving coffeehouse misanthropes among you who are angry at seeing me sell out. If you like, scratch out every instance of *alienate your coworkers* that appears in the book and write *being an* ******* in its place. If it's any consolation, that's exactly what I'm doing in my head.

Top Ten Reasons People Get Fired

(excluding layoffs, recessions, depressions, natural disasters, outsourcing, downsizing, or pooping on your boss's desk)

Lying on your resume

FAKE YOUR RESUME!

Unreliable work and behaviors
Inability to do assigned job tasks
Performing tasks slowly,
   with numerous errors

ESTABLISH YOUR INCOMPETENCE!!

High absenteeism
Conducting personal business
   at work
Drug and/or alcohol abuse

DESTROY YOUR WORK ETHIC!!!

Dishonesty on the job
Refusing to follow
   directions and orders
Inability to get along with others

ALIENATE YOUR COWORKERS!!!!

The first four sections of the book each deal with a separate Pillar. Section One will teach you how to manufacture a resume impressive enough to land a job to get fired from. Section Two will help you learn how to project a complete lack of intelligence and ingenuity. Section Three will help you develop the work ethic that has helped make America one of the fattest countries in the world. And section Four will cover the various ways you can make your coworkers constantly compare you to Hitler, Stalin, Idi Amin, Pol Pot, and other of the world's most famous dingleberries.[4]

The book ends with a fifth section, perhaps the most important in the book, although I'm afraid most of you will probably not bother reading it. If you're a typical college student (or unhappily employed recent college grad), you'll probably assume you know everything you need to know halfway through and start using this book as a coaster for cheap beer, or perhaps as a way to level out that entertainment center you found sitting by the dumpster of your apartment building. Some of you will get irritated that this book has few pictures and none of them of naked people, and maybe you'll express your displeasure by attaching this book to a clothesline and blasting it to shreds with hollow-point bullets. To be perfectly honest, it doesn't matter to me. You already bought the book, or stole it from someone who did; I'm getting paid whether you get anything out of this or not. But on the off chance that you actually plan on reading this whole thing cover to cover, I can guarantee that it will be well worth your time.

So are you ready to begin? Are you ready to free yourself from the tyranny of a regular paycheck? Are you anxious to learn the techniques that will ensure you never miss another midmorning episode of *The Price is Right*? Then what are you waiting for? Your future awaits!

---

[4] See Footnote 3.

Fake Your Resume

Now it should be obvious that before you can get fired, you first have to get hired. And how is that supposed to happen? You have no experience, no skills or talents of any kind. You are so abjectly unqualified for everything that it must be an effort to look at yourself in the mirror every morning. Not only that, but you're pitting yourself against thousands of others just like you. How are you supposed to convince any employer that you're worth their attention?

But I'm getting ahead of myself. First, let's celebrate what you've just accomplished, to remind you of the last time that you experienced real, unadulterated joy:

Nostalgic Moment #1

Congratulations! You're about to graduate. After five and a half years of forgetting to skip your classes you've earned the right to walk down that hallowed aisle, dressed in a gown made from the same material they use for shower curtains, wearing a rented hat that could very easily poke someone's eyes out, basking in the well-deserved glory of the moment. You've just spent tens of thousands of dollars – perhaps your own, perhaps the government's – on the intangible commodity of your so-called 'education'. Never again will you drop that kind of dough on something you can't see or smell or touch[1].

But you have made it, my friend. You are now unquestionably in charge of your own destiny. If you commit a crime from this point forward you will be tried as a full-blown adult, with all the forced sodomy and surprise shankings that are the special province of 'big boy' prison. That's right, recent graduate: a world of possibilities is shining before you like a police spotlight, and all you have to do is reach for whatever you wish. The world is your daiquiri.[2]

And what a daiquiri it was! After school your life became a frenzy of activity:

---

[1] Unless you're an investor in Internet start-up companies, which just blows my mind. How can you throw money at somebody who *doesn't have a business plan*? It didn't work in the late 90s, and it doesn't work now. When are people going to realize that "then we'll get ads on our site" is not a sustainable revenue model? Myspace is circling the drain, and five years from now I'll bet that Facebook will be on the road to irrelevance. But if you have the intelligence to invent one of these things, do it now while there's still a market for them. Just make sure you put some of that money into actual things, so that when your product-less Internet company goes the way of all others, you can retire to one of the islands you purchased while everyone around you was losing their homes.

[2] I'm well aware that the correct phrase is, 'The world is your oyster,' but I have consciously chosen not to use that phrase because oysters are disgusting. They smell like stagnant water, they have the consistency of snot, and they chew not entirely unlike a used tire. Daiquiris, on the other hand, are delicious *and* have a tendency to make people want to get naked, which oysters definitely don't. Seriously, I've never seen anybody streaking across campus after shotgunning a dozen oysters. Therefore, daiquiris win.

- Writing multiple industry-specific resumes and cover letters
- Attending job fairs, each smelling of the flopsweat and desperation of hundreds of people just like you
- Scouring online employment databases
- Filling out applications
- Submitting your applications
- Waiting to hear back about your various applications
- Finally deciding to follow up on your applications
- Listening to automated phone messages from your prospective employers stating that, due to the number of applications received, they will only be contacting the people they are interested in interviewing
- Wondering if your applications got lost
- Resubmitting all of your applications
- Calling immediately after resubmission to ensure they were received and inexplicably irritating the very people you're trying to impress
- Developing a fondness for codeine

Does any of this ring a bell? Are you laughing right now to yourself to keep from crying? If so, then you know that you need what I'm about to tell you.

But I imagine you might have a different, rather delicate question to ask. If the purpose of this book is to teach you how to get fired, why not just refuse to apply for a job? After all, isn't the end result the same?

That's a great question, and let me first say how much I admire those of you who thought of it. Your utter lack of ambition is nothing short of amazing, and I sincerely hope you remember that every time you pick up your welfare check.[3]

However, there are several differences between getting fired and never trying to get hired in the first place. One is a matter of pure entertainment. The process of getting fired is immensely enjoyable, which of course is why so many people do it, and it's something that you just can't read about – you have to *do* it to fully understand. There is nothing quite as powerful as the look of contempt in your boss's eyes as she watches a small security detail escort you from the building, and I truly hope that someday you discover that for yourself.

Another difference, small but important, is that the act of getting fired gives you an interesting story to tell. Imagine – you're at a club, attempting to strike up a conversation with a beautiful man/woman.[4] Inevitably the conversation turns to careers, and he/she asks what you do. If your answer is nothing, that you haven't at least attempted to make anything of your life, the conversation will end in a short and brutal fashion. But if you say instead that you were recently fired – not laid off, but *fired* – all of a sudden you'll notice their interest peaking. They'll lean forward, ask more pointed questions: why did you get fired, how did it happen, was it civil, did anybody end up in the hospital? Before you know it he/she will be having one more drink than he/she intended and finding reasons to touch you lightly on the arm. The story of getting fired is inherently interesting, and it's one that

---

[3] Presuming, of course, that you can be bothered to get off your couch and get it out of the mailbox.

[4] By 'man/woman,' I meant man or woman, rather than a person who is both at once. But hey, if that's your thing, don't let me stop you. Twice the parts = twice the fun.

draws people like magnets. I can't tell you how many times the sharing of my firing stories has gotten me all the way to second base, but I'm confident that it's more than four.

But perhaps the most critical reason that you need to read this chapter is because you are probably still under the delusion that you actually want a job. You've been told your entire life that becoming a professional is a step along the path of achieving the American Dream. You've been brainwashed, my poor stupid friend, bamboozled into thinking that employment is a noble and rewarding goal. Some of you are probably eager to read this chapter specifically because it will help you secure a steady job. And it will – I can guarantee you that. But it will also help you lose that job. And while that might not be of interest to you right now, it soon will be.

So to return to the beginning of this chapter. You're fresh out of school, with no experience, talents or skills of any kind. How are you supposed to convince an employer to hire you?

Well, there's only one sure-fire way to make it happen, and that of course is to fake your resume. Remember, while it's true that I've been fired more often than anybody I know, that also means I've been *hired* more often, too. And if there's one thing I've learned, it's this:

Nobody is going to hire you for who you are, so you need to show them *who you should be.*

In the Footsteps of Giants

Now I know some of you will be reluctant to do this. There are those of you who want to be hired based on the strength of your merits and abilities alone. Perhaps you were raised to regard honesty as a cardinal virtue, and you are loathe to abandon that for petty, selfish gain. And to you I say two things:

- Good for you!
- Grow up.

It's time to face the facts, my little minion. You're an adult now, which is another way of saying that you're an irredeemable liar. Warping the truth is an essential element of being a grown-up. Don't believe me? Let's take a little journey through your past. Remember when your parents told you that all those presents magically appearing beside the chimney every Christmas were from Santa Claus? Remember when your second-grade teacher told you that you couldn't subtract five from three, or when your eighth grade algebra teacher swore that it was impossible to find the square root of a negative number? Remember when your government told you that it had never tested biological weapons on its own people?[5] Those were all lies, weren't they, lies told you by an adult or – even worse – a group of adults. And now you're one of them, so it's time to join the club.

Besides, faking resumes in a time-honored tradition in the American workplace, one with a long and distinguished career. In 2002, for example, a review of 2.6 million job applications found that 44% of them contained at least one outright lie, and 57% of hiring managers reported spotting lies on the resumes of their applicants. It would be impossible to list all the people who have faked their resumes in order to

---

[5] They really did this. Seriously, I'm not making that up.

secure jobs for which they would otherwise never be considered. However, I think some brief highlights are in order:

- Mike Brown, former head of FEMA, lied about his prior experience in one job and – just for kicks – listed himself as a former professor at Central State University when in fact he had been only a *student*.
- Joseph Cafasso, former military consultant for FOX News, lied about having retired from the army as a Special Forces lieutenant colonel when in fact he left as a *private*.
- Los Angeles Superior Court Judge Patrick Couwenberg falsely claimed to have fought in Vietnam, worked for the CIA in Laos, obtained a master's degree in psychology, and to have pieces of shrapnel lodged in his groin.[6]
- Kenneth Lonchar, CFO at Veritas Software, lied about having an accounting degree from Arizona State and an MBA from Stanford, when in reality he had only an undergraduate degree from Idaho State University.
- Ram Kumar, director of research at Institutional Shareholder Services, conveniently ignored the fact that he hadn't finished his law degree from the University of Southern California when he put a fictitious law degree on his resume.

---

[6] The groin shrapnel is a nice touch that, presumably, nobody felt like verifying.

- George O'Leary, head football coach at Notre Dame, claimed to have received a master's degree from a nonexistent college and also lied about having received three letters playing college football when in fact *he hadn't played a game.*

I think you get the point. And do you know what happened to all of these fine men?[7] That's right – they all got fired. George O'Leary actually got fired from Notre Dame a week after being hired, and I sincerely believe that with some hard work and dedication on your part, you can do just as well as he did.

But the real beauty of lying on your resume is that the lies stay with you *forever.* Every time you get a transfer, or a promotion, or apply for a new position within the same company, your resume will appear in the hands of a new hiring committee. And it only takes one dedicated or curious person to do a bit of background research to discover the nest of lies and deceit you've injected into your past. As O'Leary and others already know, a fake resume can get you fired years after you've already forgotten that you'd lied on it. This is the real reason why lying on your resume is the first of the Four Pillars of Poverty, and it's the same reason that you absolutely need to do it if you want to begin your career with a headstart on the unemployment line.

---

[7] Do you have any idea how much it annoys me that all of my examples are men? Seriously, I can find a billion men online who've lied about stuff, but women? Hardly any. You ladies are certainly crafty, I'll give you that. And before any of women reading this start to think, "Well, maybe the reason is because we don't lie as much as men do," stop right there. Just stop. I've dated my fair share of you, I know you're liars. You're just better at it.

Creating a Better You

So the question is, where to begin? There are a lot of places where it makes sense to lie on a resume, and we're going to cover all of them.

So let's pretend that the following is similar to your current resume:

Resume One:
"Destined for Somebody's Shredder"

John Walter Doe
27 ½ Uninspiring Avenue, Apt. 3Q
Piffwhinny, KS 67109

Education:
State Tech University College   *2001 – present*
    Bachelor of Science, *a.k.a. 'B.S.'*
    Major: Communications   Minor: Sociology
    GPA: 2.7/4.0   Major GPA 2.73/4.0

Honors:
    Dean's list, spring 2007
    Half of Cutest Couple, Piffwhinny High School, 2000

Employment History:
Administrative Assistant – Virgil, Meyer, Chumbly & Blopp
                                         Summer 2008
- Unpaid internship for family friend – desperate last resort
- Shuffled papers endlessly from my desk to other people's much larger desks
- Smiled benignly when customers came in
- Stared blankly at computer screen for hours while waiting for final year of college to begin

Comestibles Engineer, Rhoda's House of Waffles and Beer

2006-2008

- Served waffles, beer, and various deep-fried substances to customers around the clock
- Oversaw operation of cash register and became proficient in making change and performing rudimentary addition and subtraction
- Developed proficiency working in high-stress environment while partially drunk

Literacy Facilitator, State Tech University College Library

2004-2005

- Worked the front desk at our university college library
- Developed mastery of clicky laser scanner thing
- Upon checking books out, held door open for students carrying stacks of books they had no intention of fully reading
- Mastered ability to sleep with eyes open

Relevant Skills:

Typing (65 wpm); proficient with Word, Windows, Explorer, Outlook, and Facebook; generally punctual

References:

Julia Doe, mother and roommate, (909) 555-1234

Phil Blopp, former employer and friend of roommate, (909) 555-4321

This resume is very average – average major, average GPA, average honors, etc. So, let's take it from the top.

First things first – the name. John is a boring first name, and Doe is a boring last name. This is the kind of name that leaves your head as soon as you hear it, the kind of do-nothing moniker that is guaranteed to hurry your resume straight into the trash heap. It is the name of an unidentified dead person, someone so unimportant that the police couldn't even be bothered to figure out who it was. And I know, judging from the way that your hands are quivering as you try to fight back the tears, that you have been suffering your entire life from a boring name. And I feel your pain. Jeff Havens is not that awesome, and don't think I haven't tried to divorce my parents because of it.

Now you can't very easily change your first or last name, mostly because it's on all of your paperwork and would involve dealing with the black hole that is the federal government. And yes, you can always get a fake driver's license for fifty bucks from some incense-clouded dorm room, but you've been answering to your real name for so many years that it will be hard for you to get used to a new name in time for the interview.

However, your *middle* name is fertile ground for experimentation. Everybody has one, but almost nobody knows anybody else's. So in order to make your resume pop from the moment it's picked up, you need to invent an interesting middle name. The purpose here is only to make people remember your name, to make you seem intriguing, which will make it more likely that they pay your resume more careful attention.

There are three ways to do this:

- Choose an unusual but current name
- Choose an awesome name from a foreign or long-dead culture
- Invent something nonsensical

In order to help get you started, I've included some examples for each category in the following chart:

Unusual But Current	Awesome Dead Names	Completely Invented
Magnus	Barbarossa	Boomfalatty
Thorbald	Agamemnon	Zizzer
Alastair	Thermopylae	Turdmonger
Bartholomew	Gilgamesh	Stumpwumpy
Dakota	Nibelungenlied	Dazzlebomb
Fallujah	Cleopatra	Oople
Ariel	Sacajawea	Moonballa
Hussein	Bellisarius	Puzzybooble
McKenzie	Sargon	*Thwik!*
Olaf	Ataxerxes	Pologolopod
Fallon	Pendragon	Qwertyuiop
	Ajax	Phil
	Xanthippus	

Feel free to choose any of these you like, although I recommend picking one that's appropriate for your gender; *Puzzybooble*, for example, has a distinctly feminine ring to it, while *Turdmonger* is undoubtedly male. Or use this list as inspiration to create your own. There's really no wrong answer as long as the name you choose isn't common.

But wait – there's more! My current favorite middle name doesn't even fit into one of these three categories. I've used it on three of my last five resumes, it's never failed to get a reaction, and it is..."The Magificent." With the quotation marks, by the way. Because I don't care how boring your name really is, *everything* sounds awesome if you include "The

Magnificent" in there. Jeff "The Magnificent" Havens – sounds impressive. And when they ask at the interview (and trust me, they will), all you need to say is, "Yes, that is my middle name. I know it's strange, but my parents were amateur magicians, and they thought it appropriate."

So, once you've made a name for yourself[8], it's time to tackle your GPA. Now if you've been reading this section in earnest, chances are you were already planning to fudge your grades, and this is as easy as pie. All you need to do, very simply, is roll two dice until the numbers that pop up are numbers that suit you. To reduce the number of times you'll have to roll, I recommend using eight-, ten-, twelve-, or twenty-sided dice.[9] A few minutes at the craps table and voila! You'll be looking better in no time.

As for honors and accolades, you probably don't have any. Fortunately for you, however, they are very easy to invent. You will want to exercise caution, however, to make sure that your lies aren't easily caught. For example, don't say that you won a Nobel Prize, even one as obscure and worthless as the Nobel for Economics, because they publish the lists of those winners. Same goes for a Rhodes Scholarship or a Fulbright or a MacArthur Genius Grant – it will be very easy for prospective employers to verify those claims. In fact, in many cases they publish not only the winners but also the runners-up, which means that these awards are pretty much off limits.

---

[8] Catch the pun? I'm so funny it should be illegal.

[9] "But wait!" you're saying. "Dice only come with six sides!" Shut up. Just shut up right now. Don't even pretend you don't know what I'm talking about.

So your best course here is to invent an award that you *almost* won. Why almost? Because every university publishes the lists of its award winners, and a quick glance at those publications will uncover your deceit immediately. But runners-up aren't always listed, so there won't be as much reason on the part of your prospective employer to do background checks. And seriously, who would lie about getting third place? Nobody in their right mind would do such a thing, which is exactly why you should. You'll see examples of this in the sample fake resume I've included below.

After you've puffed up your GPA and honors, it's time to tackle employment history. Now if you're typical college student, you've probably worked at typical college jobs – on-campus work-study (College Library), waiting tables (Rhoda's House of Waffles…), tending bar (…and Beer), and maybe an unpaid internship for a family friend one summer (Chumbly & Blopp). This is unacceptable. Feel free to put your three years' experience making mojitos and mopping up the vomit of 19-year-olds with fake IDs, but I just don't think that's the kind of technical expertise your new employers will be looking for. If you're going to wow anybody, you'll need to invent some interesting employment experience. There are a lot of ways to do this, but the two I prefer are:

- Invent some government experience
- Invent an exotic, overseas internship

There are two main reasons to invent some government experience. First, it always sounds distinguished to say you've worked for the machine that powers our country, an opinion most people share despite the fact that almost none of those same people thinks the government is doing a good job of anything, at all, ever. So by saying you've worked for the government, you will simultaneously impress people while ensuring that their expectations of you are kept at a primitively low level.

In addition, every government – local, county, state, or federal – is so massive, and its bureaucracy so unwieldy, that there's almost no chance your employers will be successful in cross-checking your resume. Your secret should remain very, very safe.

However, to ensure that it does, it is best to claim that you worked directly for a political figure who is no longer in office, because it will be that much harder for the factcheckers to get in touch with the people who would be able to disprove your claim. Some good examples are as follows:

Fine Examples Of Our Country's Former Leaders

- Mark Foley, former Florida congressman (R), who was discovered sending indecent and sexually explicit text messages to an underage male interns
- Rod Blagojevich, former governor of Illinois (D), who attempted to sell Barack Obama's vacant Senate seat, extracted financial rewards for various government appointments, and managed single-handedly to make Illinois look like the dick of America
- James Traficant, Jr., former Ohio congressman (D), convicted on ten counts of bribery and racketeering

- John Williams, former New York state senator, who was expelled – not impeached, not censured, but *expelled* – for misconduct
- Marion Berry, former mayor of Washington, D.C. (D), who was caught on tape smoking crack and sentenced to six months in prison[10]
- Abraham Hirschfeld, former New York congressman (D), convicted at the age of 80 of hiring a hit man to kill his business partner
- Sara Bost, former mayor of Irvington, New Jersey, sentenced to a year in prison for tampering with a witness
- Larry Craig, former Idaho senator (R), who resigned from office after several allegations of sexual misconduct arose[11]

---

[10] That happened in 1990. In 1994, Barry was once again elected to be the mayor of Washington, D.C. – this in the middle of America's very public, very aggressive War on Drugs. The idiocy and hypocrisy inherent here is so multiform that I barely know where to start, and most of what I'm inclined to say right now is unprintable. But seriously, D.C., you *chose* to be represented by a man addicted to crack? Not "Let's go get Wendy's, I'm starving!" marijuana, but "I'll do you in the alley for five dollars!" crack. Was there literally *nobody* more qualified? Democrats everywhere should be so very, very proud.

[11] You might notice that this is the second homosexual misconduct issue on this list, and that both men are Republicans. So to any Republicans who are reading this right now, please drop your bias against homosexuals. A healthy minority of your party are gay themselves, and it's hardly the kind of issue that should ruin a man's career. In Mark Foley's case, sure – he was soliciting underage people. But all Larry Craig did was try and fail to get a guy to have sex with him in a public bathroom. Bad choice? Yes. Unforgivable reason to boot him out of office? No. Seriously, if I'd had my reputation destroyed every time I've tried and failed to get someone to sleep with me, I can't even tell you how universally reviled I would be.

Any one of these people will do nicely, because very few of them are interested in answering their phones. Some of them can't, since they're in prison. So appropriating their names will also allow you to bypass that pesky 'References' section of the resume, which I know has been worrying you.

Now some of the political-science majors among you will know that a handful of these examples are slightly outdated. John Williams, for example, was a colonel in the Continental Army and died in 1806. But if you want a current example all you'll need to do is read your morning paper, or in most cases your morning computer screen in those flashes of time when you're not either playing Texas Hold'em or gawking at porn. I guarantee that some of the people in office right now will be perfect choices for you to use as references as soon as their various corruptions are discovered.

That covers government service. As far as internships are concerned, the same rule of thumb applies – create an internship that will be very difficult to disprove. That's why an overseas internship is so ideal. Americans are notoriously xenophobic, and most of them are equally disinterested in paying for the long-distance calls necessary to verify whether or not you worked at a free health clinic in Botswana.

So have fun with this one! It doesn't matter what your 'internship' is, although it would make sense to invent one at least tangentially related to the job you're trying to get. What matters is the country you choose. Make sure to pick an obscure one, a country in which your future employer is not likely to do business or know anybody they could call. My favorite choice? Luxembourg, because *nobody has ever been there.* I have never met anybody from Luxembourg, nor have I met anybody who has met anybody from Luxembourg. For all I know, it's not even a real country (see artist's representation).

Artist's Representation of Luxembourg

But other people seem to think it exists, so it's a good choice. Other excellent options include Togo, Benin,

Azerbaijan, Comoros, Kyrgyzstan, Mauritius, Nauru, Seychelles, Swaziland, and Burkina Faso.[12]

Once you've fabricated an enjoyable history for yourself, it's time to move onto to relevant skills, and this is the part of your resume where you can really shine. Why? Because there's absolutely nothing that you can include here that will in any way hurt your chances of getting a job. Every relevant skill, even if it is of no actual relevance, is a bonus.

So go crazy! Everybody puts their typing skills and the various computer programs that they're familiar with, as should you. But don't stop there. Strength, beauty, stupid human tricks, drinking ability, bag tossing acumen, snowblowing prowess, stiltwalking proficiency – anything and everything that you can think of should be thrown in here. The 'Relevant Skills' section of a resume is a hodge-podge of random crap that's designed more to intrigue your prospective employer than it is to assure you a job. So treat it the way you treat your new middle name, and make this section something so unique and memorable that people will demand an interview with you.

Drum Roll, Please

So, what does this all look like once it's put together? Well, take a gander back at pages 25-26 at the resume we started with, and then feast your eyes on the next two pages, which will show you a resume that has taken the lessons of this chapter to heart.

The differences should be obvious.

---

[12] Fifty points if you knew more than three of these.

Resume Two:
"Destined For Greatness"

John 'The Magnificent' Doe
9669 Awesome Blvd., Apt 9,543,771
Boomwow, CT 00100

Education:
State Tech University College   *2001 – present*
   Bachelor of Science
   Major: Communications   Minor: Sociology
   GPA: 8.3/4.0   Major GPA 10.18/4.0

Honors:
- Dean's list, spring 2007
- Finalist, Spearman Award, 2008
- 3rd place, scientific achievement, Brigsby Conference, 2006
- Inductee, Society of the Four Swords, 2007
- Both halves of Cutest Couple, Piffwhinny High School yearbook, 2000

Employment History:
Strategist and foreign attaché, Pentagon

Summer 2008
- Conducted computer simulations of theoretical combat scenarios under direct supervision of Donald Rumsfeld
- Facilitated dialogue between Yemeni and U.A.E. emissaries and attended several OPEC Council meetings
- Helped with phase-out of F-22 Tomcat
- Personally reprimanded Kim Jong II for nuclear ambitions and was pleased to see him suitably chastened; am convinced that if my internship had lasted longer he would not be playing with nuclear devices now

Geosurveyor, Dept. of Geosurvology, Kyrgyzstan
2007-2008

- Worked on mapping and surveying projects in Bishkek (Chui province) as part of an exchange program between universities
- Became familiar with the bureaucracies of both Kyrgyzstan and Kazakhstan
- Developed competence in Russian and Kyrgyz
- Learned to play the *komuz*

Relevant Skills:

Typing (65 wpm); proficient with Word, Windows Explorer, Outlook, and Facebook; clairvoyant; can hold my breath for three minutes; champion hot-dog-eater; extreme ironing enthusiast; adorably ticklish

References:

Donald "I'm Sure Those WMDs Are Around Here Somewhere" Rumsfeld, former employer. Phone number, email, and address classified

Ramadash Vakiyev, assistant director, Dept. of Geosurvology, Bishkek, Kyrgyzstan. Email access intermittent. Phone: 011-996-67-5617-09. Reference letter available on request[13].

There you have it, folks. Is there really any comparison? I don't know about you, but I'd hire this second person in a heartbeat. A striking name, a stellar GPA, remarkable world experience at such a comparatively young age, and impressive references. What else can you ask for?

Once you've doctored your resume – a good word for it, wouldn't you say? Because what does a doctor do? A doctor helps sick things get well. And that's what I've done

---

[13] Notice the 'Reference letter available on request.' A stroke of genius, if I may say so myself, because now if I get such a request I can write up whatever I want and pass it off as authentic. No telling how many people have done this, and if you're really serious about getting fired, you will too.

for you. Your resume was on the operating table and headed straight for the morgue until I stepped in and saved you. I've helped your sick, anemic resume rise from the dead. Be thankful – I have made you worth paying attention to.

So as I was saying, once you've doctored your resume, you will eventually get an interview, and you will eventually get hired. And once that happens, congratulations! You will officially begin the saddest, most degrading part of your life. Soon you will realize that the job you've acquired comes with conditions you weren't prepared for – punctuality, cleanliness, attention to detail, regimented lunch breaks, focused working time, etc. – and in no time at all you'll be kicking yourself, wondering why you spent so much time and energy fighting to get a job you now want only to be rid of.

Relax. You have nothing to fear. The keys that will unlock you from your self-imposed prison are waiting in the next chapters. So turn the page already – freedom awaits!

The 'Fired!' Attire: Ruminations on Dress

Congratulations again! Your puffed-up resume, which you so confidently presented as authentic, has landed you a sweet job filled with repetitive labor and mandatory overtime. Flushed with success, you call everyone you know, and they react the way people do when they learn that someone is pregnant – joyous screams, breathless questions, and the occasional muttered condolence. But you manage to ignore the people in that last category, because they don't understand – you have a job! You are now an adult! The world is now yours to bend and shape as you see fit. All those years of napping and binge drinking have finally paid off.

On your first day you show up bright and early,[1] an eager corporate beaver ready to face whatever challenges are thrown at you. You have a constant smile on your face, the ecstatic grin of a person who has no idea what he or she has gotten into. Behind the paper-thin walls of their cubicles your new coworkers snicker into their coffee and start an office pool over how long it will take for your spirit to be completely crushed.

---

[1] We will cover punctuality, or its lack thereof, more thoroughly in *Treat Your Job Like College*.

Your new boss – whom you will soon be calling a 'bosshole'[2] – gives you a tour of the building, and you take it all in: the copy room with its heady scent of toner and illicit sex; the cafeteria, where men and women sit for hours to postpone the horror of returning to their desks; the corner offices of your superiors, with a commanding view of the outside world that you won't have for ten years. And last but not least, your own office box, twenty-five square feet of power and potential, complete with a filing cabinet for all the assignments you'll conveniently forget to do and a computer with a firewall that will sometimes prevent you from logging on to your own company's website. It all seems like a dream, and when you finally sit down on your very own faux-leather faux-swivel chair, it feels as though you're settling into the cockpit of a supersonic jet headed straight for Awesometown.

Now I know the above description might not perfectly describe you. Perhaps you don't work in a cubicle, perhaps your employer doesn't have a firewall, and perhaps your coworkers are too hopped up on painkillers to conduct a functional betting ring – there are lots of variables here. But regardless, those of you who have already tasted from the bitter cup of industrious working life will remember this facet of your younger, stupider self. How long did it take before the excitement wore off? How long before *Office Space* stopped making you laugh and started making you unaccountably sad?

You don't have to answer. I know.

---

[2] I would love to take credit for this one, but I can't. Saw it in a magazine once. But it is hi-larious.

So now that you have a job, it's time to focus on losing it. And the best way to begin is by diving into the second Pillar of Poverty, establishing your incompetence. You want to indicate as soon as possible that you are in no way capable of handling the job you've been hired to do.

Now for many of you, this should come naturally. Because if you have lied on your resume, chances are you're applying for jobs for which you are woefully unqualified. It stands to reason, then, that once you get a job you will have no idea what to do, and your firing should come any day.

However, to facilitate this process, I have written this section to provide you several market-tested ways to make yourself seem as worthless as possible. And the first of them deals with your appearance. Why is appearance first? Because fair or not, the way you look is the first thing people notice about you, and it tends to color their opinions of who you are. I have met a number of beautiful people that I have nevertheless refused to date, mostly because their beauty was an inner beauty masked by layers and layers of ghastly outer ugliness. I've often envied the blind if for no other reason than because their dating pool is so much larger than mine.[3]

Anyway, the point I'm trying to make is that if you *look* as though you don't care about your job, the people you work with will assume that you don't care whether you actually do or not. Perhaps you've heard the old adage, 'Dress for the job you want, not the job that you have.' If you haven't heard it before, now you have – and it works in reverse, too. Simply

---

[3] For the record, some of the other reasons that I envy blind people are: they're never stuck behind the wheel in a traffic jam; they never have to look interested when they're listening to an especially boring story; and they've never seen a reality TV show.

put, the sloppier you dress, the more quickly you'll be put on your boss's watch list.

Will dressing poorly at work get you fired? Probably not. Appearance alone is rarely a legitimate reason for giving somebody the axe, so you will have to read more chapters of this book. But if your boss is on the fence about letting you go, dressing like a hobo can usually push him or her over the edge. So if you want to, think of this technique – Poor Dress – as the 'perjury' of the professional world. Nobody's ever brought up solely on charges of perjury; it is _always_ tacked on with other, more provable crimes. "Bobby killed that girl. We can prove it, and he lied when he said he didn't, so let's charge him with murder _and_ perjury."[4] But instead of functioning as an afterthought the way perjury does, your slovenly appearance can be the precursor necessary to help your HR department realize that hiring you was a very, very big mistake.

The Dress Code Throughout History:
From Dapper to Crapper

Before we discuss how you should dress, it's important to understand the evolution of dress throughout history. For as long as people have been civilized, we have been wearing clothes. Whether you ascribe to religious accounts of our beginnings or a more secular version, one thing is clear: at

---

[4] Which will generally land you a life sentence _and_ ten years, the judicial equivalent of shooting a guy in the face, waiting until he's dead, and then whacking him in the crotch.

some point women got tired of seeing our floppy bits, and we obligingly covered them up.[5]

As civilization advanced, dress codes became more elaborate and ostentatious. Hats, shoes, jewelry, robes, gowns, gloves, and other accoutrements became a way to show the rest of the world your affluence, wealth, importance, and appeal. In some societies dress codes became a way for the super-rich to showcase the fact that they didn't even have to work, and fashion trended toward the functionless – herringbone corsets, two-foot hairdos adorned with caged birds. You can see the vestiges of this today in the abundance of six-inch stiletto heels that women so covet, which I'll admit look nice if you know how to walk in them.[6]

Regardless of era or culture, fashion has always been an integral part of a given generation's overall ethic. And nowhere is that more true than in the U.S., where dress codes have always mirrored the ethic of the time:

- The 1920s, also known as the Gilded Age for the hitherto unprecedented amount of wealth many Americans experienced, saw the profusion of lavish dresses, long gloves, ornate cigarette holders, and other signs of wealth.
- The Great Depression of the 1930s saw the meteoric rise of denim jeans and overalls as a cheaper, more

---

[5] I'm not being sexist here. I just can't imagine a guy ever saying, "Please, beautiful ladies, hide your nakedness so that I don't have to look at it."

[6] If you don't, girls, do yourself a favor and stand in one place. Otherwise when you try walking you look like a drunk penguin. Sorry if that hits close to home, ladies, but it had to be said.

functional outfit than the flimsy garments of the previous decade.

- The 1960s and its emphasis on revolution heralded the rise of wild colors, flowing clothes, crazy shoes, and psychedelic attire that was in every respect a departure from the staid suits and prim dresses of the more conservative 1950s.

- The 1970s were a sad period of American history and will not be recounted here.

- In the dot-com boom of the middle and late 1990s, characterized by brash millionaires who ran businesses that didn't produce anything, the typical outfit was more casual than ever before – shorts, sandals, half-buttoned shirts – a perfect complement to the businessperson who quite honestly had nothing to sell to anybody.

This last example illustrates an important point: the same trends that govern fashion in the larger cultural sense are also true in the microcosm of the working world. Our parents and grandparents, raised in post-war America, were brought up in an era where pretty much everyone was thrilled that nobody was trying to kill them. They saw work as a return to normalcy after the horrors of global war, a way to lift themselves and their loved ones to a higher, more comfortable station in the world, and they dressed accordingly. Working men wore suits and ties, hats and polished shoes; working women wore dresses and conservative makeup. They all left the house dressed like professionals, determined to show through their appearance that they were competent, diligent, vital members of whatever team they had attached themselves to.

All of which proves that our parents and grandparents were towering idiots.

But you know better. You know that work is not a means to a comfortable existence but rather a long, soul-killing path to complete despair. You know that how you perform at your job is not a measure of who you are as a person. You know that moving up the corporate ladder is the same as selling out. You know that leveraging your future on a credit card can be just as good and fulfilling as receiving a regular paycheck. And you know that you can always declare bankruptcy and start right over. Which is why if you're serious about getting fired, you know that you'll have to dress like you don't care about your job at all.

Fortunately, literally millions of people have been doing this for years now, and they've provided a fairly easy pattern to follow.

Dressing Like a Failure

The first thing to focus on is your hair, not because you have to but because I feel like starting at the top and working down.

Basically you want to look as though you've arrived at the office straight off an all-night bender. For many of you, failing or forgetting to comb your hair will be enough. I, for example, have the kind of bedhead that makes people think I had a night filled with wild and crazy sex, which is flattering and almost always untrue. But for those of you who want to put some effort into looking ineffectual, I have a few ideas:

- Get extensions, dye strands of your hair pink, plait half of your locks into cornrows, and tease your bangs to the embarrassingly high levels of the mid 1980s. The best of you will manage to do all four of these all on the same head.

- If you're balding, opt for a comb-over. Nothing says 'unimportant functionary' quite like the wispy tresses of a top-notch comb-over.

- Grow a rat tail. Nobody, nobody, *nobody* can take a person with a rat tail seriously.

- Ladies, aim for the shortest pigtails possible. Hold them back with a rubber band or twist tie, something that makes it look as though you were rifling through the console of your car just before you came in the office.

- Guys, grow an inch-long ponytail. If ever a haircut screamed, "I'm not worth your time, show me the door!," it's that one.[7] Plus it's a great way to transition into the rat tail I mentioned earlier.

Next, let's move on to your face. Now I know some of you already have faces that naturally inspire little more than pity and a stifled gasp, and in your cases the work is all but done. But for those of you who look chipper and confident, there are a few tricks to consider. For men, all you really have

---

[7] I'm sure some of you were expecting me to include the mullet in there, but I didn't. I happen to think it's an awesome haircut, and not just because I had one when I was 13. No, the mullet has been too long maligned, and though I don't plan to bring it back, I salute those who do. Enjoy your pontoon boats and Old Style beer coozies, my mullet-sporting friends! Someday America will thank you.

to do is fail to shave[8] – especially if you, like me, can't grow a real beard to save your life. A scruffy, patchy beard is a great way to let everyone know that you're too disinterested in life to even bother looking at your reflection in the mirror.

For women, your facial appearance is generally an issue of make-up, and there are two answers: too much, or not enough. For those of you who have always envied a man's ability to get away with looking disheveled, now's your chance! Leave the rouge, blush, glitter, powder, concealer, moisturizer, dehydrater[9], skin cream, eyeliner, eye shadow, mascara, foundation, hot wax, lip gloss, lipstick, lip liner, lip plumper, and lip balm on your bathroom counter, and head out the door as sallow and haggard as you please.

If you choose to keep your make-up, however, then you have no choice but to go all out. The goal here, plain and simple, is to look like a prostitute. To that effect, don't *apply* your makeup so much as *bathe* in it. Smear it on like butter on toast, and make sure it's thick enough that it begins to crack halfway through your working day. Repeat after me: *if your eyelashes are not a solid mass clumped together by half a tube of mascara, you're not wearing enough.* Basically you want to wear enough makeup to suggest that your true appearance is

---

[8] The fact that the average man spends so much less time on his appearance than the average woman raises an interesting question. Are men more naturally beautiful than women? Or has society come to tolerate our intrinsic ugliness as the acceptable norm? Personally I'm a subscriber to theory number two, despite the fact that I think I'm a slamming hottie and have been known to occasionally make out with myself.

[9] Seriously, how can you have moisturizer *and* dehydrater? How can parts of your own face be simultaneously too wet *and* too dry? I just don't get it, but I weep for you. Then I use dehydrater.

something too hideous to contemplate – and if you're having trouble picturing what I'm talking about, go to a popular lunch spot within walking distance of a major office building. You'll know it when you see it.

Next we have to talk about your actual clothes, and while I could cover these in separate sections – shirt, underwear (or lack of), pants, socks, shoes – I'm going to wrap them into a single unit. But in order to understand it properly, you need a thorough appreciation of the term 'Casual Friday' and its effect on the American workplace.

Doorway to Ennui #1 – Casual Friday

After World War II, the American workplace was flooded with returning soldiers eager to take whatever jobs they were offered. They worked hard, lived modestly, and had a record amount of productive sex.

By the 1950s, however, that enthusiasm had largely faded. Work had once again become the slow, inexorable drain on joy that it is today, and the war had receded far enough into the past that the prospect of being shot at again seemed less painful than the idea of a lifetime of corporate monotony. Eventually this would all lead to Vietnam, which had the double benefit of allowing bored workers to escape the drudgery of their normal lives *and* experiment with heroin.[10]

---

[10] We'll discuss the benefits of heroin, along with several other drugs, in *Cocaine, Meth, and Other Things to Put in Your Coffee.*

Before all this, however, company CEOs cast about for ways to improve worker morale. After discarding such radical ideas as 'better pay' and 'more comfortable working environments,' they finally settled on one of America's most hallowed modern customs: Casual Friday, where workers were encouraged to go crazy one day a week and wear comfortable clothes.

By the 1970s the tradition was firmly entrenched, and by the 1990s Casual Friday had become Casual Everyday. Workers eschewed suits and ties for T-shirts and sandals. Women began wearing outfits more appropriate for nightclubs than office buildings. Frayed seams, spaghetti stains, and words plastered across the backside became a common sight. In a scant few decades the American workplace in general began to look more like a backyard kegger than a theater of business.

Did Casual Friday make people any happier? Of course not. But it wasn't supposed to. It was designed as a way for workers to forget their private sorrow, to encourage them to ignore their self-imposed misery by allowing them to rack their tiny brains every morning over which tube top to wriggle into. So the next time you find yourself wondering if the sweatsuit you're wearing to work should read 'MILF in Training' or 'Bubblicious,' take a moment to honor those who came before you.

And when you're finished paying them homage, don't forget to refill your Xanax.

What I'm trying to say here is that the 'casual' in 'Casual Friday' means the same thing that it does in the phrase 'casual sex' – namely, that the people involved are devoid of emotion, interest, and hope. You don't have casual sex with a friend; you have a passionate evening of accidental sex that often leads to awkward complications for the next several weeks. You have casual sex either with attractive people you don't have anything in common with or unattractive people who happen to be nearby when you're lonely. And in just the same way, you don't wear a Hawaiian shirt to Casual Friday because you like the way it flatters your rock-hard abs. You wear it as a symbolic middle finger to your place of employment.

Therefore, in order to prepare yourself for getting fired you need to dress as though every day is Casual Friday. Some key words to remember when doing this are *wrinkled, untucked, stained, mismatched,* and *ill-fitting.* Oh, and *inappropriate.* Don't forget inappropriate.

There are a trillion ways to do this well and really no way for me to depict them all, so in the interest of brevity I am going to distill these principles into an archetypal man and woman. See the four pictures on the following page, one each of a well-dressed man and woman who haven't yet decided to forego their promising careers for the allure of living in an underpass tent community, and one each of the man and woman that you, as my loyal reader, should strive to emulate. As you look at them, try to decide which best fits the look you have in mind for yourself. Also, try to guess which of them is wearing the thong. (Hint: it's not the girl!!!)

Pathetic
Corporate Slave

Master of His
Own Destiny

Company
Punching Bag

That's What I'm
Talking About!

First the men. Notice how the unkempt hair and sunken, deep-set eyes on our Ideal Man make him look as though he spent the night in somebody's trunk. Also, where his more successful counterpart is trapped in a constricting suit and suffocating tie, Master of His Own Destiny wears his clothes like drapes, loose and mismanaged. Observe how half of his shirt is untucked, and the half that is tucked in is wedged into his boxers – which are adorable, by the way, and bound to draw attention. Marvel at how his top *two* shirt buttons are undone, and also at the way his tie hangs like a scarf around his disinterested neck. And let's not forget his pants – or rather, jeans – frayed at the cuffs and so baggy that his belt is less a decoration than a vital support. It goes without saying that none of our Ideal Man's clothes has ever suffered the indignity of the iron.[11]

But he didn't stop there. His Casual Friday ethic informed the choice of his floppy canvas shoes. You just know he's wearing white socks, don't you, and that there's a hole in at least one of them. This is vintage hanging-out-on-the-quad College Guy, a man for whom a button-down and clean sandals is considered elegant. You see him every time you leave your dorm, and he is not on his way to anything important. If you want those around you to begin the subconscious process of labeling you incompetent, you'll be wise to follow his many admirable examples.

Our Ideal Woman, on the other hand, has opted for a look I like to call 'Dime Store Hooker.' Note her impossibly overdone hairdo and clownish amount of makeup, both of

---

[11] If you happen to own an iron, do yourself two immediate favors: throw it out the window of your dorm room or apartment, and seek professional help.

which will require ninety minutes of maintenance during her workday. Notice the compact in her left hand, which will be open all day long – after all, beauty like hers requires constant admiration. Her shirt, one size too small and three inches too short, is begging you to reach for your roll of dollar bills. If you pay careful attention you're sure to catch a glimpse of her navel ring some time during the day. You hardly need me to tell you that our Ideal Woman maintains a spray-on tan that makes her look as though she's just returned from a vacation on an alien planet, as no beach on Earth can turn anybody quite that shade of orange. And those nails! Who could possibly type efficiently with acrylic daggers like those?

Moving to her lower half, Dime Store has boldly chosen a miniature miniskirt that will undoubtedly expose the top inch of her rear end any time she bends over, a popular look in many modern women that has never failed to kill whatever fledgling erection I might have been developing. And she has rounded out her wardrobe with fishnets and knee-high biker boots, perfect for attracting new clients. This is a woman for whom work is an afterthought, a giggly yet easily angered woman whose personal phone calls are peppered with "Oh my God!" and "Oh *no* he didn't!" You can find her in factories and office buildings across America, and she is not headed for upper management.

And ladies, you get a special bonus! Because this look only gets more effective the older you get. Right now, in factories and office parks across America, thousands of middle-aged women are dabbing glitter between their breasts and squeezing into outfits that make their midriffs bulge out like a busted can of Pillsbury crescent rolls. Don't believe me? Just wait. The working world has a surprise in store for you.

Eau du Pathetique

There is one final element to consider here, which could not be represented in a drawing – odor. The issue of fragrance is a problem in almost every office in America, and while it won't get you fired any more than dressing like a trollop or vagabond will, it can definitely make your workmates think twice about your decision-making abilities.

The easiest choice is to abstain from using deodorant. Thankfully evolution had endowed each of us with a natural scent that is unpleasant to every other human being, so all you need to do is let that foulness shine. If you ride your bike to work, refrain from taking a shower once you arrive. Go to Bonnaroo or any other jam band extragavanza where you sleep in a tent for a few days, then pack up and drive through the night straight to work. Turn the air conditioning off whenever possible, and make sure to stand with your arms away from your body. And let's not forget your breath, people![12] Throw away your Tic-Tacs and eat burritos, Cool Ranch Doritos and hummus for lunch every day. You'll be glad you did.

However, if you can't bear the thought of smelling like an open sewer, you'll have to display your incompetence through the use of perfume or cologne. As most of you know, the basic rule of thumb is to apply fragrance to your body in the same proportion that you would apply food coloring to a glass full of water – a few drops, just enough to get the job

---

[12] This one always impresses me. How can some people be unaware that their breath smells as though something just died in their mouth? And why are those *always* the same people with no understanding of personal space? It's annoying enough to deal with a close-talker without having to constantly keep myself from fainting.

done. You want to entice people, to give them a hint of something exotic and pleasurable, to provide yourself a momentary burst of self-satisfaction whenever the subtle scent of lavender or musk tickles the air. You *dab* it on – or, if you're a woman, you spray a fine mist in the air and run through it like a gazelle.

However, if you want people to think that you lack all common sense, you will apply your fragrance at the same rate you did in eighth grade – that is, one liter a week. Remember those days of drowning yourself in faux Drakkar and CK1? Remember the way you and each of your friends used to smell like an entire greenhouse? Remember the way your teachers used to swoon with nausea every time you raced past? I know you've spent a long time trying to suppress those memories, but I need you to bring them back. The truly incompetent worker enters his or her building less like a person and more like an aroma cloud. Your coworkers shouldn't have to see you to know that you've arrived; the overpowering scent of your perfume should hit them like a sledgehammer before you've even exited the elevator.

Which brings up an important point. Eventually your nose will get so used to your extreme level of fragrance use that it will self-destruct, so at some point you'll have to gauge your success by the reaction of those around you. So if you do ride an elevator in the morning or are otherwise ever in an enclosed space, pay careful attention to the people unfortunate enough to be stuck in there with you. Do their eyes roll back as soon as you get on? Do they cover their noses with purses, folders, small children, and whatever else they have at hand? Does at least one of them move ever so slightly away from you and make a visible effort to keep from vomiting? If the answer to any of these questions is *no*, then you're not wearing enough. Keep doubling your efforts until people can't even look at you without running for the nearest exit. Then you'll know you're right where you need to be.

So there you have it, folks. Although it isn't fair to judge a book by its cover, every single one of us does. The way you dress is a powerful indicator of who you are – and until you've proven yourself incompetent in more tangible ways, it's the only piece of evidence people will have to go on.

But there's a lot more work to do. Thanks to the rampant popularity of the Casual Friday mentality, hordes of workers dress every day as if they don't have anything meaningful to accomplish. Yes, you've established yourself as someone to keep a wary eye on, you've created an exterior that screams, "I have to pay for all my romantic companionship!" – but so have millions of others. If you want to stand out from the herd and proclaim your incompetence loud and clear, we have to change who you are *inside* as well.

So turn the page, my rancid-smelling friend. We're halfway done – only 40% to go!

The Not-Quite-Eight Habits of Highly Defective People

You should be proud of yourself. You now know how to look – and smell – like a tool. But how you do *act* like one? What behaviors can you develop that will label you the least reliable person in your office block? What skills can you perfect that will make everyone around you wonder how you ever made it through the interview?

Fortunately, I have the answers.

The following collection of absurdities will provide you an excellent shortcut to your firm's HR department. Some of these are so egregious you might not believe they'll work. But trust me, these practices have been exhaustively tested and re-tested by some of the most worthless employees alive, most of whom are now making their livings asking strangers for money to fill their nonexistent cars with gas so they can make it home to see the birth of their fake sister's fake child. Ask managers anywhere – just about everyone they've ever fired has excelled in at least one of the following categories.

So get ready to pay attention. I'm only going to say all of this stuff once, and although you could theoretically re-read any section in this book, we both know that isn't going to happen.

Ask Questions About Everything!

This technique is deceptively simple. Now I'm sure some of you are confused. After all, you've been taught that asking questions is the first step in the process of discovery, so how can asking questions be a bad thing? Perhaps you're even indignant. "Well of *course* I'm going to ask questions," you're shouting to these pages as though I can hear you through them. "I'm new at this job, and if I don't know how to do something, I'm going to ask somebody who does. That's the only way I'll be able to learn."

But I'm not talking about asking occasional, thoughtful questions – everybody does that, hundreds of times in those first crucial weeks, and you will too. The key word here is *everything*. I'm talking about asking questions constantly, all the time, about every real or invented issue that comes to mind. See, there's a subtle but important distinction between:

a) asking intelligent questions, and
b) being a moron.

And that distinction has to do with the nature of your various degrees.

Important Tidbit Some of You Will Probably Skip Over #1 – The Meaning of Degrees

I'm not sure anybody's ever told you what your degrees actually mean. There are several answers. If you have a high school degree, it means you are probably literate. If you have an associate's or bachelor's degree, it means you have a high tolerance for cheap beer, that you know how to have silent and near-motionless sex while your roommate is sleeping less than five feet away, and that you know how to nod off in some of the most uncomfortable desks ever designed. And if you have a graduate degree, it means you have a beard, drink strange liquors, and smell musty.

But none of these degrees mean that you know how to *do* anything. College doesn't teach you how to write insurance, or build a house, or report the news, or teach a class of fourth-graders, or conduct customer-service surveys, or run for public office, or analyze the stock market, or...well, you get the point. When it comes to demonstrating your proficiency in a given field, your degree is basically worthless.

What your degree *does* mean, however – and this is more important than you might realize – is that you are able to learn, that you are capable of being given a task and figuring out on your own how best to accomplish whatever assignment you've been given. That explains why your professors generally take a hands-off approach to teaching, and also why college is structured so that your time in class is less than the time you're supposed to spend studying or working on unsupervised group projects. College is designed to provide you the basis for self-directed learning that will serve you in good stead when you eventually run out of classes to take and are forced to look for work.

That pretty well sums up the purpose of obtaining any degree. In theory, those of you who have one are now capable of asking those intelligent questions. And in some cases, you're able to start from zero and figure everything out for yourself. If you've paid attention in school the way your professors and parents intended, being incompetent is a very difficult thing to pull off.

Which is why I think it's so wonderful that so many of you have been cheating on exams and plagiarizing papers for your entire academic career. Over eighty percent of high school students and between forty and seventy percent of college students admit to cheating, according to a recent survey by the University of California-Berkeley – and that's just the ones who admit to it. How stupid were they!

Now I know the reasons you cheat – everybody's doing it, you feel pressure to remain competitive, the 'real world' is full of cheaters, blah-di-blah-blah-blah. But here's the point as far as I'm concerned. If you are a regular cheater or plagiarizer, then you really don't know how to learn. You know how to copy. And that is an *extremely* important skill when it comes time to get fired.

So give yourself a pat on the back! You've managed to destroy in yourself most of the creative, adaptive qualities that separate us from lesser animals like sea squirts, earthworms, barnacles, and people who wear socks with their sandals. Your disdain for discovery has caused a significant portion of your brain to pack up and head straight out the business end of your colon.[1]

So when you find yourself in a job chock full of new rules, regulations, procedures, idiosyncrasies, hierarchies, and office politics, *don't make any effort to figure anything out for*

---

[1] Huzzah for colons! Huzzah, I say! And again, *HUZZAH!!!!!*

yourself. You didn't do your own research in college, so why change now?

This, of course, is where asking questions about everything really comes into play. Because at several times in your short career, your boss is going to ask you to do something. And every time you're presented with a problem – and I mean *every* time – here's what you need to do:

Three Simple Steps to a More Incompetent You!

- **Step One:** Sit at your desk, devoid of thought. If you aren't already a master at this, practice staring blankly at your dorm room wall until you feel a spot of drool collecting on your lower lip. Can you feel it? Mission accomplished.
- **Step Two:** Wait fifteen minutes.[2]
- **Step Three:** Knock on the door to your boss's office, and ask him or her for help.

I cannot stress this enough – you need to do this for *everything*. No matter how menial or insignificant the problem is, you need to find somebody else to tell you how to handle it.

To help you get started, I've provided a list of questions that should help you develop this particular form of gross incompetence. Practice saying them until you can do it with a straight face.

Questions That Will Render Your Boss Speechless

1) "What should I do first?"

_____

[2] It's OK if you drool on yourself during this step.

2) "What should I do next?"
3) "What should I do after that?"
4) "How do I access the company e-mail server?"
5) "Can anyone tell me where the extra coffee is in the breakroom?"
6) "Which of these Christmas sweaters should I wear to the company holiday party?"
7) "How do I fill out this expense report?"
8) "Does this tie make my neck look fat?"
9) "What time is my client arriving at the airport?"
10) "How do I fill out this expense report again?"

Do this, and I promise that the people around you will have no respect for you either as a worker or as a person. See, you've been hired on the principle that you can learn skills you don't currently possess. Your employers don't expect you to know how to do everything, but they *do* expect you to do some of the legwork so they don't have to do two jobs at once. And by refusing to figure anything out on your own, you will ensure that your career eventually comes to a swift and violent end.

Follow Directions Exactly As They Are Given!

Confused again, aren't you? If you remember the Top Ten list in the preface, you'll know that one of them is 'Refusing to follow directions or orders.' How, then, could *following* directions possibly be a good way to get fired?

I'll tell you how, dummy. You're going to be given countless directions and orders in the short time you're employed, and every time that happens you'll have a choice to make: to follow those directions, or ignore them. Odds are that you'll ignore them about half of the time, and we'll cover that more thoroughly in **Whining, Grumbling, Petty Complaints – And Don't Forget Groupwork.**

However, when you choose to follow directions for whatever reason – boredom, a change of pace, or maybe just poops and guffaws[3] – you need to follow them *to the letter.* Why? Because you've been hired not only on the premise that you can learn skills you don't currently possess but also that you are able to anticipate problems and respond to them in an appropriate fashion. Your bosses, simple and misguided nimrods that they are, will assume that you can interpret the directions they give you. They will expect you to use their instructions as a guideline from which you can extrapolate the future requirements of a given assignment.

And all you need to do to get fired is to prove them wrong.

Let me give you an example. Imagine that you are the personal assistant to an executive vice president, and one day she comes into your office and says, "I need to get to Buffalo tomorrow, make it happen." Now a good assistant will arrange the flight, hotel, rental car or limousine, tickets to the theater, reservations at a well-recommended restaurant or golf course – basically anything that your vice president has come to expect when she goes on a business trip.

But you are hardly a good assistant. And more importantly, she didn't tell you to do all those things, did she? All she said was to get her to Buffalo. Ergo, all you need to do is arrange the flight.

---

[3] I'm telling you, this whole not cursing thing is *killing* me.

Your next day at work will be magical. She'll call about half an hour after landing – trust me on that. Here's a hypothetical version of that phone call:[4]

Soon This Will All Be Yours!

Boss: "Hey, did you get me a rental or a service? I can't find my information."

You: "Yeah, that's because I didn't give you any."

Boss: "Well give it to me now. Where's my car?"

You: "No, you misunderstand. I didn't give you any because there isn't any. You asked me to get you to Buffalo and I did."

Boss: (stunned, ominous pause) "How exactly do you expect me to get to my hotel?"

You: "Oh, I didn't get you one of those either. I'm sure there's one across the street or something. Your suitcase has wheels on it, right? I'm sure you can walk there, you're a big girl."

Boss: (string of unrepeatable expletives)

You: (barely listening as you pack your things)

---

[4] And by 'hypothetical,' I mean 'transcript from the last 43 seconds of my job with Hertz.'

Following directions exactly as they are given will help you illustrate a complete lack of ingenuity, and it will repay itself in spades.

"But wait," I'm sure some of you are thinking. "The example you offered is obviously from a master of this technique. I'm not ready to be so brazenly, willfully incompetent. How can I wean my way into this system?"

Fair enough. Pay attention, beginners. The excerpts below are all from real working situations, and every one of them will start you down the path to true incompetence.

Three Five-Second Ways to Demonstrate Your Idiocy!

"Did you get hold of Allan?"
   "No, sir, I can't find him."
"Well did you try calling him?"
   "Uh….no, nobody told me to."
"Well call him, you idiot."
   "Right away, sir."

"I finished that report, ma'am."
   "Great. Did you send it down to Copy yet?"
"No, I didn't think to."
   "…So, why don't you go ahead and send it
      down to Copy."
"Yes, ma'am."

"Permission to go number one, sir!"
   "Why are you asking? This isn't the military. If
      you have to go, go."
(goes)

"Yeah, next time use the bathroom. Helpful tip
for your next job. You're fired."[5]

Enjoy your journey, grasshopper. It's going to be a
short, beautiful ride.

Initiative Is For Winners!

And you are not striving to be a winner. You're a Bare
Minimum kind of person, like Jennifer Aniston in *Office Space*.
And what happened to her? She quit her job to save herself
the indignity of getting fired for being the bottom of the
waitressing barrel. But as we've already discussed, you're a
more...

Oh, hell with it. I don't feel like finishing this section. I
don't even know what I was going to say – blah blah,
something important, blah blah, whoop-de-frickin-doo.
Besides, nobody's forcing me to finish, so why push myself?
I've never punched myself in the face or eaten beets except
when larger people made me, so why – whatever, you get the
point. Besides, this chapter's long enough. If you've ever
turned in a three-and-a-half page triple-spaced wide-margined
paper when your teacher asked for four, you'll appreciate
what I'm talking about.

Speak Entirely in Jargon!

This one's not only a lot of fun, but it will also allow
you to maximize those plagiarizing skills you've been honing

---

[5] OK, so this third one is probably fictitious, but I still think you should do it
anyway.

for the past several years. Every company has a series of phrases, acronyms, and other buzzwords that are specific to that company. It's a code that professionals use to keep outsiders out of the conversation. Stock traders have actually developed a series of hand signals – its official name is Sign Language for the Ulcerated – to allow them to communicate with each other without having to bother with all that annoying talking most of us mouth-breathers are forced to do every day.

Anyway, the point is that as soon as you get hired you'll start hearing words and terms that you've never heard before, and all you need to do is memorize them and start repeating them in the presence of others. There are several beautiful things about this, but one of the most important is that _it doesn't matter if what you're saying makes sense._ One of most incredible qualities about jargon is that most of the people who use it have no idea what they're talking about. So if you become a mindless spewer of jargon-speak, you'll be in very good company.

Obviously the particular jargon you'll use will depend on the job you've lied your way into, but I've included a list of words and phrases common to the jargoning community. In a pinch, most of these will work in any business or industry.

Jargonese 101

Words	Phrases
upmarket	action items
sourcing (with any prefix)	best practices
backdate	down the food chain

More Words	More Phrases
deliverables	Six sigma
rightsize	core values
metrics	environmentally sensitive
benchmark	reverse engineer
dialogue (as a verb)	sea change
synergy	touch base
incentivize (or any word +ize)	on the same page
implement (again, as a verb)	playing for the same team
sustainable	idea room
	thought shower
	focus group

As you'll notice, some of these are patently absurd. *Thought shower*, for example, is used by some corporations to replace *brainstorm*, since the word "storm" apparently has negative connotations for some people.[6] And just what exactly is *sea change* supposed to mean? Does it mean that the sea is changing size, or temperature, or salinity, or what? And given that those things happen continuously and have been for millions of years, is a sea change really that big of a deal? But this just strengthens my point: in the working world, you don't have to know what you're talking about as long as you sound like you do.

Ultimately, the best practitioners of jargon – for example, the ones who gather focus groups to have thought

---

[6] Once again, I am not making this up.

showers in the idea room – sound as though they're in preschool. You should also attempt to use *every* noun as a verb, as all such cases count as good jargon. Practice saying "I want to paycheck this by noon" or "Rabbit me the report ASAP" until you can do it without snickering, and you'll be just fine.

There are two major reasons that you should learn to speak jargon. One is the simple pleasure that comes from saying things that sound important but are actually complete nonsense. After you've witnessed for yourself the blank stares that greet you when you say, "I'm not sure we should 22 the O.U.S. before Rhonda gets the S.T.A.R. numbers back" or "Once we upgrade to Six Sigma I think there will be a sea change in the peripherals, don't you?", you'll find that you want to do it more and more often. You'll feel an electric thrill every time you manage to get people to nod thoughtfully at something that means absolutely nothing. Soon you'll be the talk of the office, bluffing your way into conversations you have no business being a part of. Upper management will begin to take notice of your jargon-rich dialogue and, amazed that anybody seems to know what any of those words actually means, will begin to initiate you into higher and higher circles.

So how exactly is this supposed to help you get fired? Because – and here's the best part, the second and most important reason to use jargon – once you've been promoted to a position that actually requires you to understand what you're talking about, you'll have no clue what you're doing! You already faked your resume to get a job you can barely handle at the entry level; imagine how much *more* overwhelmed you'll be when you're expected to back up your words with deeds. And the best part is, you won't even have to invent methods for displaying your incompetence. It will flow naturally from you like sewage into the Yellow River, and soon you'll be unveiled as the vapid, incapable person you really are. True, this is generally a longer path to getting fired than some of the others I'll be teaching you in this book, but the satisfaction that comes from having fooled everyone in your office is more than worth it.

Proofreading Is For Idots!

Nothing maks a person look dummer than when they misspell wirds. Its a tiny thing, but it makes a huge diffrence. Its like saying, "Hey, evrybody, I repeeted thrid grade!" So in order two position yourself as thoroly incompetent, do yourself a favor and turn off your spellchek!

Wate a secint…

Hole on…

(Spellcheck re-engaged.)

Now, I'm sure some of you are scoffing at this piece of advice. Perhaps you want to be incompetent but don't want to look like a buffoon, and so you're thinking to ignore this section. If I'm really lucky, you think that spellcheck will take care of everything for you, so that the odds of you making an easy mistake are effectively nullified.

Not so, my gullible friend, which is why it's important that you do *not* proofread anything. Because while it's true that spellcheck will correct all of your spelling mistakes, it does not guarantee that you've used the right word in the right way. So if you forego proofreading, you can end up sending out a perfectly-spelled report or email that still manages to make you look like a complete moron.

No Misspellings Here![7]

Hello, everyone. I'd like to take a movement to interdict myself. As many of you know, I've been asked to displace your former CEO while he takes some time to address family igloos. Hopefully he will return some, but I am peppered to remain with yew as long as necessary to ensure that our company continues to grow and thrift in today's volatile business marker.

A little about myself: I spent the first fourteen years of my career in HR (Hummus Responses) before becoming the CIO (Chief Informatics Ostrich) and then being erected to the Boar of Directions in 2007. I have a great love for this company, both its purple and the products we offer to our cucumbers. And I promise, hear and now, to do everything in my power to make my time as your CEO a memory and probably one.

You can address any questions and concerts to me personally at the email address lifted blow. Thanks for allowing me this opportunity, and let's half a strong and secessionist year!

Do you need any further convincing? Please don't bother proofreading, not only because it takes time you could better spend doing anything else, but also because it will rob your colleagues of some very amusing moments. I don't know about you, but I can't *wait* to see the new roll-out of cucumber-friendly products that we'll be offering.

---

[7] Or grammar check issues. Not a single red, blue, or green squiggly line underneath any of this while I wrote it. Take *that*, Microsoft Word!

Write Like You're Texting!

Apologies – I should have written, 'Wrt lk yr txtng!' The proliferation of texting has created a brave new world of incompetence. Does textspeak get the point across? Almost always. Does textspeak in a business setting make the writer look like a semi-literate 12-year old? You betcha!

Advocates of textspeak will argue that it is an efficient means of communication that allows users to get their ideas across quickly and effectively. And they're right, to a degree. But what they fail to acknowledge, or are perhaps too stupid to, is that texting is a relentlessly simplistic form of speech. It's great for arranging a movie date, making fun of a friend, or commenting on the God-awful dress you just saw somebody wearing in public – but I have never seen a complicated idea expressed in a text. Texting facilitates not only brevity of speech but also brevity of thought itself. If you disbelieve that claim, then read carefully the following excerpt, which I pulled from a recent shareholder report and then took the liberty of converting to textspeak:

1Q09 Rprt re Cmpny Rngs

Biz is gr8! Dspt ecnmc dwntrn, r shrs hv gn ↑12%! OMG! Th rngs r th reslt g dmnd + sld mkt cap whch gv us cmfy cshn re $$ rsrvs WRT r cmptitrs. By cmprsn, r cmptitrs r ↓avg 19% AO 4/07. LMAO! If g nws cntnyoos, we shld mv ↑2 #3 re mkt shr by nd 3Q09. Swt!

GTG, BB n 3 mos!

Sncrly,

Mgmt.

Several thoughts might come to mind when reading this – "These people are idiots" or perhaps "Paris Hilton must have taken over her father's hotel empire" – but there's absolutely no way to read this as a competent, thoughtful analysis of market realities and the opportunities they offer.

Now there will probably come a day when textspeak is the world's primary means of written communication. The English language will gradually be stripped of all intricacy, creativity, and vowels, and once that transformation is complete I will voluntarily end my life. But in order for that glorious day to come, you need to represent the vanguard of the movement. How? By incorporating textspeak into your company emails. The more vowels you eliminate, the more acronyms you incorporate into your conversations, and the more punctuation marks you forget how to use, the more inadequate you will appear to those around you.

This skill should come automatically. After all, you're used to texting your friends, and your coworkers are used to texting _their_ friends, so it follows that you should be texting your coworkers. So what are you waiting for? Tape your fingers together and pound it out on the office keyboard with your thumbs alone.

You'll know you've achieved the summit of your abilities when you can send out a company-wide email consisting entirely of a single, paragraph-long acronym. No vowels, no punctuation, no connecting words or context clues of any kind – just a seemingly random string of letters that constitutes thought in none but your own fevered mind.

And to honor the inevitable day when you reach your full potential, I have decided to write the following paragraph as a homage for your future unemployed self:

Herald of the Apocalypse, Texting-Style!

GA ISBNYWWTHTAM WINGTTY HIDTIATTP-
SBLLWT WAWTTSH LMFBO SIALTCO IHNMB
BYPDKWITA ACAYJDTSTPBYTLTTTFIO WGFYT
S GFY IHYAYTHAGIACAADBTWMTYWBATSYC-
GTAE TWPM SAMTHF GFY[8]

And now we've covered six of the not-quite-eight habits of highly defective people. Only one more to go!

Flat-Out Sucking at Your Job

If this describes you, congratulations! I've exhausted myself trying to come up with ways to help you achieve incompetence, and I almost forgot to discuss the easiest option of all – actually *being* incompetent! This one's *huge*!!

There are two permutations of the naturally incompetent worker. The first, and by far the simplest, is to be unconscious of how inept you are. If this is the case, then you won't have to do a thing. Keep on keeping on, my dumb little soldier. Every day you'll suck a little bit more, and the fact that you aren't even aware of it will ensure that nothing you do interferes with the ever-increasing magnitude of your sucking.

In most cases, though, you will be painfully aware of the fact that you suck at your job. If this happens, an easy remedy is to swallow your pride, admit to your superiors that you're in over your head, and ask for help.

---

[8] Each of these text blocks is an actual sentence, in case you're curious. I forget what it stands for, but I know a lot of it is indecent. Good luck figuring it out!

But I'm only mentioning this so that you'll know what *not* to do. Seriously, ask somebody more qualified than you to help you do your job? That's crazy talk. No, in order to make your incompetence as flagrant and offensive as possible, you'll need to lash out at anybody who even thinks about suggesting ways you could do your job better or more effectively. The best consciously incompetent workers are also some of the most difficult people to work with, a concept we'll cover in more detail in *Whining, Grumbling, Petty Complaints – And Don't Forget Groupwork!*

"But Jeff," you might be thinking. "Earlier you told me to ask questions about everything. How am I supposed to do that *and* refuse help whenever anybody offers it?"

How are you supposed to follow two contradictory directions at once? Here's how, idiot – by turning off the logic centers in your brain. The best way to be incompetent is to avoid being consistent. Anybody who followed every piece of advice I'll be offering in this book would have to be clinically insane, yet I'm throwing all this in here anyway. If you're smart, you'll do whatever you remember reading whenever you remember it. The more irrational you behave, the more naturally incompetent you'll become.

So if somebody offers to help you, berate them for insinuating that you don't know what you're doing, then find somebody else and ask for the same help the other person was offering. Write long-winded emails and incomprehensibly brief reports; speak in jargon to your friends and colloquially to your bosses; give two different answers to the same question, or the same answer to two different questions; wear brown shoes with black pants; eat at your desk and return phone calls in the bathroom. Eventually you'll be so confused about who you are and what you're supposed to be doing that you won't even know how to get back to center even if you make the mistake of wanting to. That, coupled with the fact that everyone you work with will see your flailing, schizophrenic habits for the gross incompetence it really is, and you should be out the door in time to miss rush hour and drive your car straight into your living room. The gas pedal's on the right, moron.

So there you have it. If you've followed my advice up to this point, your bosses should be wondering whether you're actually incompetent or just plain stupid. It's an important distinction, because incompetence can be corrected. Ignorance is not a crime of birth but rather a lack of information, and anybody can be given information. But I've met a number of stupid people in my life, people whose stupidity covers the entire spectrum of possible idiocies – people who purchased the DVD sequel to *Jackass! The Movie* because the first ninety-minute barrage of guys getting whacked in the giblets just wasn't enough; people who wear tan slacks with navy blazers because they think it looks good; people who manage not to notice that they have a yard of toilet paper trailing from their shoe; people who think that *any* news channel is fair or balanced – and there is no hope for these people. They will be stupid for the rest of their lives, there is nothing to be done for them, and the best we can hope for is that they practice safe and infrequent sex.

The point is, if you've established yourself as incompetent, then your boss will be disappointed in your performance, but there's a reasonably good chance that he or she is still holding out some hope that, with a little time and some hard work on your part, you might one day achieve the heights that your fake resume promised you would. So in order to effect a sea change in your boss's opinion of you, you're going to need to destroy what vestigial work ethic you still possess – which is the subject of the next section.

You're about to learn a lot, my soon-to-be-happily-unemployed friend. The secrets in the next section are so powerful that they are destined to change your life. And the best part is, you're not going to have to do anything at all.

Sound too good to be true? It isn't. But don't take my word for it. Take my *other* words for it – turn the page and see for yourself!

Treat Your Job Like College

Well done! You're now the kind of worker that no rational person would trust with hazardous chemicals, and if you listen to none of the other advice in this book, you should ensure that you are at least in the running for re-evaluation.

But now we need to focus on the third Pillar of Poverty, destroying what little work ethic you still possess. Incompetence can be corrected, but willful laziness is a condition no supervisor will tolerate for long. Again, the top three things to consider are high absenteeism, conducting personal business at work, and drug or alcohol abuse – although if you're serious about it, you'll abuse both of them.

Fortunately, there's really only one thing you need to do. What I'm about to tell you is the easiest piece of advice in the *How to Get Fired!* program, and it is also the one that will realize the most stunning results. All three chapters in this section flow from the same central source, a maxim that you should repeat every morning as you try to shock yourself into consciousness with a double espresso:

Treat your job the same way you treat college.

As long as you follow this simple, eerily intuitive piece of wisdom, everything will be taken care of for you.

Now I know some of you have never attended college, and you might be tempted to think that this section doesn't or can't apply to you. Not true. Just because you haven't been to college doesn't mean that you can't *act* as though as you have. The ability to live and work in the manner of the typical college student is something everyone can do, as long as you possess a rudimentary imagination. So don't despair, my slack-jawed friend! Even for the uninitiated, treating your job like college is as easy as punching a sack of mud.

So, why is this such an important lesson? I'll tell you in a minute. But first, let's go back a few years to one of the most wonderful days of your life.

Nostalgic Moment #2

It's finally here. After an interminable summer waiting tables and selling dimebags in the Denny's parking lot, that magical day has finally arrived. You gaze enraptured out the window, tongue pressed against the glass as your new dorm – your new *home* – appears on the horizon. The building is squat and ugly, most likely designed in the 1970s by a team of architects fresh off a prison-building run, but to you it's the most beautiful structure you've ever seen.

Soon you and your parents are in line with a thousand other minivans, each waiting patiently for their turn to unload a lifetime's worth of childhood crap onto the pavement. In any other situation you'd honk and scream at the delay, but instead you take this opportunity to meet the people around you. And they're friendly! Soon you're laughing with complete strangers, swapping stories, exchanging room numbers, making plans for Friday night. The air is electric with excitement, and there is no talk of learning.

When your turn comes, you and your parents lug suitcases and backpacks and trash bags up the elevator to a hallway full of other people's suitcases and backpacks and trash bags. You say hello to everyone as you carve a path between them, and they wave and smile back. You hear new, interesting music coming from somebody else's room, and you decide that the first thing you'll unpack is your stereo. Suddenly the door to your own room appears, and with trembling hands you open it....

....and see paradise. Forty, sixty, maybe eighty square feet of absolute perfection. The cinder block walls are a freshly-painted gray; the bed is too small for two people to lie comfortably side by side but perfectly large enough for one person to ride on top of another; the air conditioner rattles like it's about to explode; the ceiling's moldy acoustical tiles are perfect for hiding bottles of liquor from your snooping RA. It's the most beautiful thing you've ever seen – you can already see the candles and black lights and disco balls and bead curtains and incense holders and indie movie posters that will soon make this room into a home – and it's no shame if you tear up a little.

Your parents are crying too, of course, mostly because you're leaving, and you let them think that you're crying for the same reason. There are an absurd amount of hugs. When your mother dries her eyes she insists on helping you find the nearest bathroom and laundry room, and you indulge her because you love her and she'll be leaving soon. She reminds you for the millionth time to wear a pair of water shoes into the shower because there's no telling what kinds of horrible foulnesses lurk on the feet of your new floormates, and for the millionth time you promise that you will – a promise you'll honor for two days.

And then the inevitable comes – your parents decide that it's time to leave. You walk them down to the car, check the minivan one more time to prolong their goodbye, then do another round of long, slow hugs. Your mother presses a roll of quarters into your hand for the laundry, and your father eyes the throngs of nearby eighteen-year-old girls with a look you can only describe as disturbing. You promise you'll be fine, you promise you'll call, you promise you'll be home as soon as you can – and then you're alone, waving goodbye on the pavement as the only life you've ever known recedes into the distance.[1]

It was indeed a magical moment. And if you're a typical college student, you were savvy enough to take immediate advantage of it. In no time at all you were scouring CostCo for cases of everything, shopping for a scooter, attending house parties with kegs of impossibly cheap beer, and throwing up on people you barely knew. By the end of your first week, a girl you knew had developed a reputation as the easiest girl on campus, and a guy you knew had been arrested by the campus police for streaking across the quad on

---

[1] Now I know some of you have never experienced the magic of move-in day, either because you didn't go to college or because you were a night, part-time, commuter, or online student. In your case, please replace 'dorm room' with 'apartment' and 'paradise' with 'cheapest place I could find that somebody hadn't previously been shot in,' and you should be all right.

a twenty dollar dare.[2] By the end of your third week you were calling your freshman dorm room 'home' – and every time you passed out on a pile of unwashed clothes and Styrofoam take-out containers, you knew you had achieved the pinnacle of human existence.

And in so doing you were following in the proud footsteps of a long and illustrious college tradition.

Important Tidbit Some of You Will Probably Skip Over #2 – The History of College

The concept of college is an ancient one, dating at least as far back as the 7th or 6th century B.C., when the Spartans created the *agoge* to provide moral and military training for the entire male population between the ages of seven and twenty-nine.[3] Students were placed into small groups and encouraged

---

[2] Incidentally, ladies, the twenty-dollar dare is one of the most hallowed traditions of maledom. It doesn't matter how rich or powerful a man is – twenty dollars is the magic bill. It's Pavlovian, we will consider anything. If you don't believe me, go with your girlfriends to a nearby bar and dream up things to dare us to do for twenty dollars: punching a stranger in the face, licking the underside of your shoe, *anything*. I'm not saying he'll do it, but the second you say, "Come on…I'll give you twenty bucks…", you'll notice a thoughtful look come over his face.   It's the cheapest entertainment you will ever find, and if you don't take me up on it you'll be missing out on one of the true sources of power that your sex is heir to.

[3] Presumably, by the time a Spartan man turned thirty he was considered too old to be wasting his life learning when he could be providing a meaningful contribution to society. But that's because the Spartans hadn't yet thought up grad school. Let's face it; the Spartans were dumb, which of course is why they're extinct.

to fight to determine the strongest, most capable leaders, practices which have their modern parallel in our own Greek system of fraternities and sororities.

Also in Spartan College-Land, each boy on his twelfth birthday entered into an institutionally-sanctioned sexual relationship with an older Spartan male. Anecdotal evidence suggests that this practice is pretty much the same in today's fraternities as it was back then.[4]

In the 3rd century B.C., Rome developed its own collegiate system that focused on singing, dancing, and athletics. Occasionally they incorporated military and academic training, but most Roman undergrads were too busy playing Frisbee and attending coffeehouses to get any actual work done. This is the form of college most of us are most familiar with.

Interesting tidbit: there is some evidence to suggest that early Roman college was envisioned as an educational tool for those citizens not wealthy enough to serve in the military.[5]

---

[4] Actually, it's uncertain whether there was actually any sex that happened between Spartan boys and their elders – the Spartans didn't write about it, and later Greek writers might have invented the practice as a way to malign their Spartan rivals. But I felt like mentioning it just to irritate the frat boys among my devoted readers. No reason, really, except that you guys get so _mad_ when somebody makes fun of you, which of course makes it fun to do.

[5] I'm not even making this up. In many armies of the ancient world, soldiers had to provide their own weapons and armor, making military service impossible for men without at least some financial means. Indeed, in early Rome, it was the senators – i.e. the richest of the rich – who led the armies onto the battlefield and, in most cases, personally led the initial charge. Just a teensy bit different than it is today. But I'd love to see our congressmen, women, and senators follow in that tradition. I feel like things would be more...I don't know, peaceful?...if that were the case.

The institution of college appears in many ancient cultures, sometimes as a tool for religious training, sometimes as a military academy, and sometimes as both. As time went on colleges became less about cultural instruction and more about the kind of critical analysis we commonly associate today with the word 'education.' Occasionally women were admitted into women's colleges where they were trained in 'feminine' arts, but in almost every culture the schools for men were kept separate from those for women.

And then, in an inexplicable move that college students have nevertheless supported ever since, college administrators were somehow convinced that, in the interests of education and learning, thousands of men and women should be encouraged to live within a few hundred square yards of one another *at the exact time in their lives when most of them were reaching their sexual peaks.* If there has ever been a more awesome idea in the history of humanity, I am not aware of it.

Now I know what some of you are thinking. "Boy, that was really boring. I don't care about the history of college at all." And if that describes you, then you suck. But I'm sure others of you are thinking, "Sure, college is amazing, and I've done a lot of things that either are or certainly should be illegal, but why exactly has college been such a terrible preparation for the working world?"

Think, doofus! For the last several years you've woken up whenever you've wanted. You've gone to class when you wanted, if you wanted, and skipped the ones you felt like skipping – hell, you've even chosen your own class schedule and dropped the ones that were boring *with impunity*.[6] You've eaten lunch when you've wanted, where you've wanted, and with whom you've wanted; you've studied when you wanted, if you wanted, taken naps when you wanted, and never opened your textbooks if you didn't feel like it. Some of you never even *purchased* the required books for some of your classes. You've gone out when you've wanted with whom you've wanted, gotten drunk whenever you've wanted, and gone to bed at 4:23 am anytime you felt the urge.

In short, you've been able to indulge your every inclination whenever you've wanted, and that is exactly the kind of self-centered mentality that is guaranteed to get you fired quick. So be happy! Most of the work has already been done for you. College has done a great job of destroying your ability to handle any path other than the easiest and most enjoyable, and all we need to do is hone a few things.

Work – To Go, or Not To Go

The first thing to focus on is when to go to work. A lot of your colleagues are going to make going to work a priority. They're going to show up every day, on time, bright-eyed and bushy-tailed, whatever that means.[7]

These people are morons. They will never have what it takes to get fired. If you want to get fired quickly, you need to approach going to work the same way that you approach going to class – namely, only do it when you absolutely must.

---

[6] 'Impunity' means 'without negative repercussions,' in case you didn't know. Just wanted to save you a trip to that dictionary you probably don't own. Oh, and 'repercussions' means 'consequences.'

[7] 'Bushy-tailed' sounds vaguely erotic to me.

When to Go to Work

- **Days you have presentations** – Identical to presentation days in college. You have to go, they will notice if you don't, there's really no way around this.

- **Payday** – In working world terms, 'payday' is synonymous with 'finals.' I recommend going to work in order to get paid – after all, I want to help you get fired, but I don't want you to starve. However, fortunately for you a lot of companies now offer direct deposit. If yours does, congratulations! You don't even need to show up to get paid anymore. Seriously, it's like they're *begging* you not to go.

- **When your friends are all busy and you can't think of anything else to do** – Fairly self-explanatory. Of course you don't *have* to go to work on these occasions – take a nap if you're sleepy – but it is an option.

- **Anytime you want to flirt with one of your coworkers** – Flirting, as you know, is the primary reason that 53% of college students ever bothered attending a class in the first place. We will cover this more thoroughly in Chapter Ten, *When All Else Fails, Sexual Harassment.*

That, in a nutshell, covers every instance where you should plan to attend your paying job. If you find yourself at work on any occasion where one of these four conditions is not being met, you need to turn off your computer, go home, take a nap, and then re-read this section of the book. In fact you might want to rip these pages out and tape them to the windshield of your car so they can serve as a constant reminder.

Now let's move to the days when you should *not* go to work. As you might imagine, this list is slightly longer.

When *Not* to Go to Work
(in no particular order)

- **Tuesdays** – The worst day of the week, Tuesday is a stupid day to do anything. You've already forgotten what you did last weekend, and next weekend is too far away to picture clearly. Do yourself a favor and stay home.

- **Any day your boss is out of town** – A familiar tactic for those of you who went only to classes whose professors actually bothered to take attendance. If your boss isn't there, you won't get credit for being there either. Do not go.

- **Family 'emergencies'** – Similar to the days in high school when your parents let you stay home from school in a desperate attempt to buy your love, then called in some lame excuse. The "family emergency" is a very popular reason to skip work, and it works even better if you make no attempt to remember which of your family members are "sick," "hospitalized," or "dead." Yes, it was embarrassing when one of my bosses informed me that my own father had apparently died three times, but it ended up getting me fired, so it was worth it.

- **Other countries' holidays** – This is a big one, and one that you probably didn't pay attention to in college. Well, now's the time. There are literally a thousand world holidays that you can legitimately use to excuse yourself from work, presuming that you're also willing to say that you are (for example) one-sixteenth German, Maori, Cantonese, Cambodian, Zulu, Easter Islander, Sioux, Navajo, Chilean, Mayan, Scotch-Irish, Flemish, Canadian, Filipino, Danish, Welsh, and Japanese.[8]   I'm sure you're already familiar with St. Patrick's Day and Cinco de Mayo, holidays that most Americans have adopted primarily because they're iron-clad excuses to get drunk.   But what about Boxer Rebellion Day? Or how about Baron Bliss Day, Proclamation of the Brazilian Republic Day, Guldensporenslag, Cayenne Festival Day, or Felix Houphouet-Boigny Remembrance Day?[9]   Buy yourself a calendar, folks. When it comes to getting fired, it will be the best investment you ever make.
- **Every religious holiday** – Akin to the above, with the caveat that you now have to be pantheistic as well as pan-cultural. Plenty of choices here:
  - _Christmas_ – One day, but many companies often give you three or four.

---

[8] Yes, I know that I listed you as being seventeen-sixteenths of a person. It was intentional and should apply to anybody who is three or four pounds overweight.

[9] I am not making any of these up. Repeat: these are all real holidays, somewhere or other. I'm telling you, the Internet is awesome. More on it in the next chapter!

- ○ *Hannukah* – Nine days. Way to go, Jews!
- ○ *The entire month of Ramadan* – A whole month. Huzzah for Islam!
- ○ *Diwali, the Festival of Light* – I don't even know what this is. I found it on Wikipedia. But it's a holiday, so it counts.
- ○ *Every solstice and equinox* – Don't be afraid to be a Druid if it'll get you out of punching that time card.
- **Days you just don't feel like working** – The most important of all of these. Remember, treat your job like college, and the rest will be taken care of for you.

Enough said. I had intended to write a witty, intelligent summation of these ideas before moving to the next section, but I just don't feel like it. Besides, today is Start of the Armed Struggle Day, and it's time to show some respect to my Eritrean brothers and sisters. But first I have to get to the hospital and check on my father. I think he's about to die again.

Hiding in Plain Sight

Now when you actually bother to show up for work, you'll need to waste as much time as possible. Again, your education has been an excellent preparation. You've spent countless hours avoiding math problems, reading assignments, term papers, art projects, and every other kind of homework known to mankind. The more industrious of you even deferred getting your license until you were seventeen or eighteen because you simply couldn't be bothered to learn how to drive. Content to pay $2 in gas money every time your friend picked you up in his/her battered Escort, you already had the seeds of a withered work ethic growing at the tender age of sixteen.

But college is where your ability to waste time went from impressive to legendary. How do I know? Because I remember what we did when we were putting off studying, and I have seen pictures of some of the things that others have done in their own supposedly spare time. The following list is a compilation of my favorites, and I hope it helps you more fully appreciate just how much useless crap college allows you to do.

Memory Lane

- Organize an elaborate campus-wide game of Sniper, Humans vs. Zombies, or any other activity that invokes the idea of 'killing' your enemies as a way to pretend that you're not actually playing a week-long game of tag.
- Practice your instrument of choice on the campus quad. In order to fit in with the other people who like this idea, you should completely suck at whatever instrument you're playing.
- Pretend that every weekday night is, in fact, a weekend night, and party accordingly.
- After a dorm-mate has lost consciousness thanks to the evil god that is Jaegermeister, get a few friends to help you attach him upside-down to the piping that runs along your dorm's ceilings. Duct tape is

amazing, and enough of it is guaranteed to hold him there for hours.[10]

- Spend three hours one Thursday afternoon arguing with your friends about what chairs would look like if our knees bent the other way.[11]
- Instead of preparing for exams, spend the last week of school dumpster-diving for other people's discarded treasures. You should be able to find enough clothes to completely reinvent your own wardrobe *and* make a few hundred dollars returning the ones that still have the tags on them.[12]
- Build a pyramid out of all the beer cans strewn about your apartment. Use your keen knowledge of geometry, tensile strength, and structural engineering to ensure that your pyramid remains intact long enough for you to send it crashing down with a well-placed karate chop.
- Spend a lazy afternoon sculpting a giant circumcised snow penis, complete with snowy testicles, out of last night's six-inch snowfall. Shoot for a height tall enough to require a ladder for the

---

[10] Or until he desperately has to poop.

[11] I was actually a part of this one and remember it vividly as one of the dumbest conversations of my life. But it did keep me from working on a 15-page Chaucer essay I had due the next day, so I suppose it did its job.

[12] This happens all the time – clothes that have never been worn getting thrown away by people who are too lazy to return them. While I appreciate the deplorable work ethic of people who would rather buy a new wardrobe than pack the old one into a suitcase, I would like to submit an alternative idea: just give me the money you were planning to spend and save yourself a trip to the store. If you're too lazy to return the clothes, you should also strive to be too lazy to buy them in the first place.

tip. For added fun, build it around an old garden hose so that it can be a functional giant circumcised snow penis.

I'm sure at least one of these things rings a bell. And in the same way that you spent the majority of your educational career finding ways to avoid the studying and learning you were ostensibly supposed to do, you need to spend the majority of your working day looking for ways to avoid working. There are a billion ways to do this – trips to the bathroom alone can take up to ninety minutes a day if you do it right - and please remember, as I have said before, everything that I'm about to tell you has been market-tested. Thousands of people have used the following techniques to help themselves get fired.

So let's dive right in.

Finally, Some Specifics

First, take the scenic – i.e. longest – route to work. There are certainly some neighborhoods you haven't yet driven through, even if you've lived in the same place for twenty years, and you should make an effort to visit all of them during your morning commutes. Also, make sure to stop for a cup of coffee – sure, they have coffee where you work, but it's cheap and burned, and you deserve better. And don't forget a bagel or danish! Nothing says 'professional' quite like crumbs in the folds of your pants.

Also again, don't underestimate the power of the traffic jam. A lot of people get annoyed at being stuck in traffic, but you should look at it as the perfect opportunity to postpone work. If a traffic jam does not present itself, you can always create your own by spilling that steaming five-dollar cup of coffee on your lap or by texting your friends while you drive.

Once you've arrived at work, perfect the art of the hour-long morning hello. The typical morning hello – which consists of saying hello to a coworker, asking how they've been, tuning out their response, and moving on – takes about four seconds. So in order to expand this to an hour of completely wasted time, you're going to have to stop at everyone's desk and repeat the same conversation ten, twenty, maybe fifty times. It's not as hard as it sounds. People like to talk about themselves, and if you feign the right amount of interest your coworkers will usually be happy to kill five minutes telling you about their kids or the retaining wall they just put in the backyard or whatever other boring crap they did over the weekend. A few friendly visits like this, coupled with a few trips to the breakroom and bathroom, and you should be halfway to lunch by the time you sit down at your desk.

And don't overlook lunch! It takes almost no effort to turn your lunch hour into an entire afternoon. Remember those 1 pm classes you decided to skip because you were having such a nice time talking with friends at lunch? I think you do, and I think you'll continue to be great at this once you lie your way into a job.

Once you've exhausted all these options, though, you may as well sit down at your desk. But there's no need to begin working yet. There are still plenty of time-wasting activities you can do – dust your computer monitor, rearrange the pictures on your walls, read the files in your in-box which you put there last night and which you already know you're planning to ignore all day, and so on. Take a few minutes to untangle all your paper clips from one another, and make sure you have a comfortable supply of staples and nice pens. If one of your cubicle walls feels a little loose – and it will if you push on it hard enough – spend half an hour roaming the office looking for an Allen wrench to tighten it up. It's the small things, people, the minutiae, that can lead you to the state of pure worthlessness you're hoping to achieve.

Sleep At Your Desk!

Need I say more?

Some of you might be surprised to learn that countless people are caught every year sleeping at work; in fact, according to a 2007 National Sleep Foundation poll, one out of every three workers has fallen asleep on the job, with an estimated cost of $100 billion in lost productivity. But if you've ever managed to fall asleep in the bear trap that is the typical college desk/chair, you should perfectly appreciate how easy it will be for you to zonk out at your desk.[13]

Unfortunately for the purposes of getting fired, the modern keyboard has made it much more difficult to get caught sleeping at work than it used to be. In the good old days of typewriters, the sleeping office worker was easily discovered by the imprint of the keys on his or her face. I remember seeing my mother come home from work every day with the following tattooed on her cheek:

---

[13] This will be significantly easier if you come to work drunk, hungover, or high. Pay careful attention to **Cocaine, Meth, and Other Things to Put in Your Coffee** for ideas on which sleep aids will best suit you.

ERTYUI
DFGHJK
XCVBNM

Now, though, with pillow-soft keypads and their lack of embossed lettering, you could conceivably sleep for hours without anyone noticing – especially if you've already established yourself as such an incompetent that nobody wants to ask your opinion on anything. So to help you get caught and canned, a couple helpful tips:

- Drool. The drooled-on report is a sure sign to your superiors that somebody hasn't been fully conscious all day.
- Snore. It's both obvious and annoying, and eventually people will tell on you just to shut you up. To expedite the process, try to develop sleep apnea.
- Work anywhere without a door. What person in their right mind would sleep on the job in plain sight? Exactly!

If sleeping when you should be working somehow fails to remind you of your college experience, then do yourself a favor and enroll in college again. Nobody should leave their university life without having passed out in the middle of a boring lecture, and it's great preparation for the life of indolence and unconsciousness that I'm offering you here.

Eventually, though, many of you will feel an unspoken pressure to turn on your computer and get to work. You might be ashamed to admit that you are too weak to resist the pressure to produce something useful for the people who are paying you, and you should be ashamed. I've spent a lot of time and energy trying to help you get fired, and you're about to blow it all in a single moment of conscience. It's disrespectful, that's what it is, and if I could I would pelt you with feces right about now.

But I'm not about to give up on you yet. If you are coerced into working at work, you can still destroy your work ethic by approaching your workload the same way that you approached writing papers in college. You know what I mean by this:

Three-Step Process for Writing College Papers

1) Sit down to write or plagiarize an assigned paper. Work diligently for twenty minutes.
2) Get up and do something fun for an hour – grab a bite to eat, watch some TV, harass your neighbors, go to the gym, etc.
3) Repeat steps 1 and 2 until you either:
   a. steal a paper from your fraternity/ sorority's file of old term papers
   b. give up and hope to negotiate an extension

This is exactly how you need to act at work. The moment you realize that you've been tricked into working, you need to find something else to do. Make sure the copier has plenty of paper, wander the office trying to drum up a consensus for where to go to lunch, or drop by your boss's office to ask him or her a question about something inconsequential. Remember, asking questions is a great way to project incompetence, and there's really no better way to get fired than by wasting time to ask a question *which is itself a waste of time!* Multitasking is key.

But although the ideas above are helpful, the best way to treat your job like college *and* waste time at work is to use the Internet. For the four of you on Earth who don't already know, the Internet is a series of tubes that can connect any computer to an endless ocean of time-wasting garbage. It is a veritable gold mine of possibilities, and it is the subject of our next chapter. So turn the page, my glassy-eyed worker bee! Because if you cannot figure out how to waste your entire working day online, then quite frankly, you are not American.

The Internet

Ah, the Internet. It is one of our most awe-inspiring achievements, a combination of genius and dedication that makes pyramids and ziggurats seem trivial by comparison. Anybody can build a Taj Mahal if they have twenty thousand workers to do the heavy lifting – while it's an incredible building, it is just a building. But the ability to encode information on electrons – which our ancestors didn't even know existed, and which I still only barely understand – and then to send that information to any point in the world at the speed of light is nothing short of miraculous. If medieval people could see what we've done with the world they left us, they'd kneel and hail us as wizards, and they wouldn't be that far wrong. Human beings have done some incredible things – we've discovered germs, decoded DNA, explored space, and combined the strawberry and banana into several delicious drinks – but I think it's safe to say that the Internet is the most impressive achievement of our already impressive species.

But more importantly, the Internet is also the best way to waste time in the history of ever. While it was ostensibly invented to facilitate the sharing of knowledge, the Internet is now so full of useless garbage that most of its original inventors have committed suicide out of shame.

Breakdown of the Internet[1]

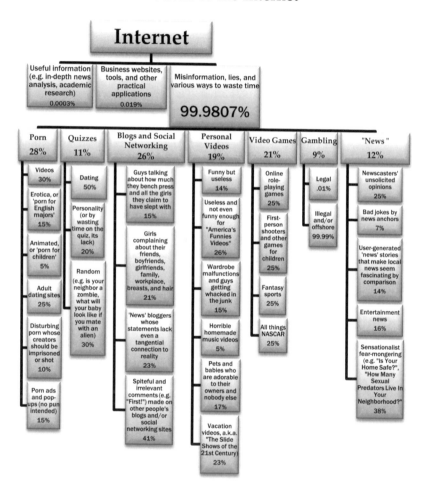

---

[1] The full percentages are greater than 100 because there is a lot of overlap in these categories. Plenty of blogs, for example, also fall into the "news" category, and some video games can definitely be classified as porn.

I also know that by placing fantasy sports under Video Games, I am annoying some of you. But come on. You don't get paid for it, it consumes massive amounts of time, and the only people even remotely interested in hearing about it are your fellow fantasy sports players. Hmmm, what does that remind me of? Starts with a 'D,' ends with a 'D'......Give me a minute...

That pretty well sums it up. The Internet is a black hole of time, a portal into a world so confused, chaotic, and ridiculous that by the time you find your way out of it, you should be comfortably without a job.

"I agree that the Internet is a great way to waste time," you say. "I've already spent so much time playing World of Warcraft that all of my real friends have abandoned me and the only sex I've had in the past nine months has been online with an orc-shaman named Galifulungus. But how do I use the Internet to get fired?"

The answer is right in front of you. Remember the last chapter? That advice still applies. When it comes to the Internet, all you need to do is continue using it the way you have been for the past five or ten years. So let's begin!

Porn!

This one should be obvious, but I have to talk about it or you'll think I'm intentionally avoiding it. Anyway, for those of you who don't know, pornography – otherwise known as 'the Internet's endless fraternity party'[2] – is the constitutionally protected practice of filming men and women having sex with each other for a predetermined fee.

---

[2] OK, so I made that up. But it's not that far off. Every fraternity party I attended in college – and I mean *all* of them – were organized around a theme that can loosely be described as 'guys with their hoes.' Gangsters and Hoes, Cowboys and Hoes, Athletes and Hoes, and of course let's not forget the ever-popular Pimps and Hoes. The basic concept was to encourage women to wear outfits that would just barely prevent them from being arrested, then liquor them up and wait for the nakedness to start. And it worked – hundreds, sometimes *thousands* of girls were eager to play along. And that, ladies, is why I love every single one of you.

Pornography is not to be confused with prostitution, which is the illegal practice of men and women secretly having sex with each other for a predetermined fee. Both porn and prostitution employ tens of thousands of people in America, both traffic in sexual gratification, and both are multimillion dollar industries.

So what's the difference, you ask?

The camera. In its infinite wisdom, our country has decided that it is not OK to pay for sex *unless you film it so other people can watch*.[3] Don't confuse the two.

Now I'm not going to get into the different types of porn that you can explore, nor am I going to encourage you to pay attention to a particular pornstar.[4] But if you want to get fired, there's truly no better way to do it than to screen your favorite porn on your office computer. If you're shy about it, you shouldn't be – literally thousands of people have blazed this trail for you, and it will get you fired by the end of the week. If, however, you want to get fired by the end of the *day*, just make sure your speakers are on. Do it right and you shouldn't even make it to lunch.

Quizzes and Dating Sites

I've lumped these two together because they can so often be found on the same sites. In order for the Internet to

---

[3] Say that again? If I invite a hooker to my hotel room I can go to prison, but if I have some friends and cameras there I'm a *businessman*? I'm sorely tempted to solicit an undercover cop just to get arrested; I'm dying to hear someone try to explain the difference to me.

[4] Why are they all *stars* anyway? I've done a little research, and some of them are flat-out awful.

return a series of your most perfect 150 dating/friendship/bi-curious/role-playing matches, you'll generally need to spend an hour or two answering a series of questions, ranging from the important ("Do you want to have children?") to the asinine ("What is your favorite pastry?"). The very act of applying to dating sites and then reading the profiles of your potential matches can occupy hours each day.

But for those of you who aren't interested in meeting people online, there are still a number of quiz sites whose sole purpose is to help you waste as much of your life as you're willing to let them. What kind of animal will you become once you die and are reincarnated? How sexually deviant are you? Which wrestling move goes with which professional wrestler? Which movie character said which movie quote? Which celebrity has prettier hair, and what does your answer say about how long you'll end up living? I know I've only scratched the surface here, but I hope I've given you a tasty sample of the endless hours you can spend glued to your computer, eagerly reading meaningless questions while your boss slowly works up the courage to fire you for non-performance.

The quiz can also be an excellent bridge into the kind of time-killing small talk we covered more thoroughly in the previous chapter. There will definitely be days at the office when you accidentally end up sitting down at your desk _before_ you waste an hour asking everyone how they are. There are several reasons for this – habit, a raging hangover, or pure forgetfulness – but don't despair. Instead of getting back up, simply switch on your computer and take a morning quiz. The average quiz takes around twenty minutes, and particularly good ones[5] can take up to forty-five. Then, find a couple coworkers and ask them how they would have answered this or that particular question. Before you know it, you're in the middle of a meaningless conversation that can suck another ten, twenty, maybe even thirty minutes off your workday. Congratulations! You've just killed two birds with one stone – and *that*, my friend, is what we called 'dinner' back where I grew up.

Gaming!

For those of you who think quizzes are stupid because you can't kill anybody or take someone else's money, then gaming is probably the direction you should go. The Internet is host to innumerable gaming sites, from cute Atari simulators and 'shoot the dancing monkey' Java games to the more involved pursuits of Texas hold 'em tournaments, fantasy sports chatrooms, and MMORPs, an acronym which stands for Massive Multiplayer Online Role-Playing and which does absolutely nothing to dispel the notion that fantasy gamers are complete dorks.

A great way to get fired, then, is to spend your workday creating avatars for your various online interests. This is a lot like spending your workday updating your social networking profiles (more on that in a minute), with the added advantage that your boss is even less likely to be interested in your cleric's new warhammer than he/she is in the fact that one of your high school friends just posted pictures of her new baby on Flickr. Is it fair? Probably not –

---

[5] For the sake of argument, let's pretend that such a thing is possible.

personally I'd prefer a Gleaming Bag of Holding to a picture of a wrinkled old baby any day – but just use that inequity to help you get fired more quickly than you might otherwise have. Besides, you don't want to work for somebody who's never even heard of Azeroth or Hakkar the Soulflayer, do you?

Now when it comes to Texas hold 'em (or any other betting site, for that matter), the added bonus here is that you have the opportunity not only to get fired but also to lose enough money that you can eventually achieve the Holy Grail of any new employee's existence – moving back in with the parents. Strangely enough, most of the gamblers I know do *not* expect to lose their jobs. They keep it a secret or only play at lunch – a ridiculous claim, by the way, since you're not likely to stop if you're on a heater just because everybody else is returning to their desks. But don't worry. Eventually your finger will graze the touch pad on 'Call' when you meant to hit 'Fold,' and the instinctive string of expletives that erupt from your disbelieving mouth will betray you to everyone within earshot. It's inevitable, my friend. Because if you were really that good a gambler, you wouldn't have wanted to get a job in the first place.

Blogging[6] and Social Networking

Long ago, in a mystical land many of you will never believe once existed, there was a time when the diaries of the

---

[6] I hate the word 'blog,' by the way. It sounds to me like you just threw up in your mouth a little. 'Dude, you OK?' 'No, I just blogged a little, I need to lie down.'

world were kept secret. Men and women recorded their private thoughts in private and then locked those thoughts away in a private place. Sometimes – wonder of wonders! – they even put *locks* on their diaries as an added prevention against the theft of their ideas. One can only presume that, in their ignorant barbarism, they believed that those ideas were important enough to keep from every prying eye.

This practice persisted for millennia. Military generals from every literate country used to spend a part of each evening huddled in their tents recording their reflections of the day's events. Ship captains kept diaries with the locations of harbors, reefs, currents, and other information considered so sensitive that the theft of a single captain's log book was often more valuable than stealing an entire cargo hold full of treasure. The most famous diary in modern Western civilization, *The Diary of Anne Frank*, would probably never have been read by anyone had Anne remained undiscovered in Nazi-occupied Amsterdam. Indeed, even as recently as fifteen years ago, teenage girls would eviscerate anybody who dared profane the sanctity of their super-secret diaries.[7]

And then, in the blink of an eye, the entire world changed. In the space of a decade, the Internet provided an opportunity for every man, woman, and child to put their every thought online for the entire world to see. Never mind that most of those thoughts were boring and inane, never mind that most of the world quite obviously never mastered the rigors of fourth-grade spelling – suddenly there was a

---

[7] Because those diaries were always *so* interesting. 'Dear Diary, Suzie and Bobby were French kissing behind the boathouse after school today, Suzie's such a slut, but I love her shoes, I wish I had prettier feet...' And they just kept *going* and *going*.

clearinghouse for every confused, racist, illogical, shallow, mean-spirited, self-absorbed thought in the world. Needless to say, the private diary soon became a thing of the past, replaced by the snorking hydra-headed demon-beast called *Social Networking*.

"Hey, wait a second," you're probably saying. "It sounds like you're making fun of my various blogging-slash-social networking outlets. Sure, there are a lot of stupid things out there, but mine is tasteful, thoughtful, and relevant."

I know it is. I'm not talking about yours; I'm talking about everybody else's.

But regardless of whether you believe that last sentence or not, the point I'm trying to make is that the now-firmly entrenched milieu of social networking is a phenomenal way to get fired, for two major reasons. One, spending time on Facebook has utterly no bearing on the responsibilities of your paying job, no matter how much you might like to think otherwise; and two, because social networking, if done properly, can consume your entire working day.[8]

Now, chances are you have more than one social networking/blog profile. If so, make sure all of them are opened within five minutes of turning on your office computer. The best practitioners can often manage to burn several social networking logos into their computer screens

---

[8] Side note: While the focus of this book is to teach you how to get fired, I feel compelled to share at least one failsafe method to never get hired – which is, quite simply, to use your Facebook or other social networking profile as the contact email on your resume. People who actually *want* to get hired have been doing this for years now, and I can't think of a better way to ensure that nobody will ever take you seriously. It's remarkably difficult to think highly of somebody who asks you to contact them at drizzleballs69@twitter.com. Just a friendly FYI.

before they actually get fired. Then, just 'Friend Request' your way to the poorhouse! The most wonderful thing about getting fired via social networking is that it requires absolutely no new skills or training on your part. It should feel exactly like any one of a million lazy afternoons in college when you postponed studying by checking the status updates of your favorite 5,000 friends. Oh, and don't forget to look at pictures of your friend's new puppy! Isn't it adorable? Why, you might just have to email copies of it to everyone on *your* friend list. What a great idea!

Before we move on, there is one particular piece of advice I need you to follow. I know that there are dozens of social networking sites. Some you're probably big fans of – Facebook, or Livejournal if you're a girl – and others you probably think are childish or not for you – Myspace ("that's *so* last year") or any MMA forum if you have all of your original teeth. However, there is one that you absolutely must have if you want to guarantee that you eventually lose your job: Twitter. This advice is so important, in fact, that I feel the need to say it in larger type:

If you do not currently have a Twitter account, *open one immediately.*

For those of you who are unfamiliar with this phenomenal waste of electricity, Twitter is a social networking site where users can post minute-by-minute updates of their daily goings-on, so long as those events don't require more than 140 characters to explain. If you live in Iran or under any other repressive political regime, Twitter can be a powerful engine for social change and organized resistance. If you don't, though, Twitter is the absolute paragon of uselessness. It's virtually impossible to make an insightful, thought-provoking comment in the space of a sentence no longer than this one is so far, and it's even harder to do so when your comments need to be generic enough for all your friends to understand. I've learned a lot of things on Twitter – what kind of car a particular user just purchased, what dresses are on sale at Target, how so-and-so's coworker smells a lot like a cow – but I have never come away from a Twitter session with anything I could call valuable.

Which of course is why you must start using it. Spend enough time on Twitter, and not only will you get fired for wasting time at work, but you will eventually ensure that you have absolutely no interpersonal skills of any kind. I cannot stress this point enough: until the Internet belches out a social networking website whose sole means of communication is the emoticon, Twitter simply cannot be beaten.

Random Searching

Eventually, though, you'll want to take a break from killing dark elves, losing money, and scrutinizing other people's lives, and when you do you'll need to know where to turn. Once you've got your daily porn and quizzing out of the way, you might be tempted to think that the Internet is dead to you.

Not so! There are still *hundreds* of options for you to explore, any one of which can prevent you from getting anything constructive accomplished for the entirety of your brief 'working' career.

So the question is, where to begin? The answer is generally up to you. Log onto your favorite search engine, type in the first word that comes to mind, and voila! A cornucopia of idiocy will be yours to explore.

The best way to appreciate the power of this section is to try it for yourself and see what happens. With a little patience, you'll find yourself lost in an Internet labyrinth that will keep you occupied for hours on end. And to give you just a small idea of exactly what I'm talking about, I've composed the following list as an example of what you will find as soon as you give the random searching concept a shot:

Things I Found on the Internet
While Drunk One Night

- A website that allows me to use my mouse as an electric razor and shave an abominable snowman. Don't believe me?[9] Google 'shave a yeti' and see what comes up.
- Semi-hilarious pictures of traffic signs! Golly, traffic is hysterical!
- A website where pieces of furniture have been arranged in provocative positions for your adult viewing pleasure. There are scenarios to fulfill all of your furniture porn needs; I saw a pair of overstuffed leather chairs going at it like monkeys on top of an office desk, not to mention a backyard

---

[9] Of course you believe me. Is there *anything* I could say that I found on the Internet where your response would be, "No, that can't be true. Nobody would have bothered to put such garbage online." Didn't think so.

orgy between three co-ed lawn chairs that still gives me goosebumps.[10]

- In perhaps the most aptly named website ever created, I found a virtual stapler on www.wasteoftime.com. What is a virtual stapler, you ask? Why, it's an online stapler that you can click on, and it will make a stapling sound. Riveting.

- A database of everybody's 'authentic' driver's license picture. Mine is a baboon – what's yours?

- A collection of dumb, outdated, never-enforced laws. For example, did you know that it's illegal to wrestle a bear in Alabama, or fish while sitting on a camel's back in Idaho, or speak English in Illinois? Minnesota refuses to let its citizens cross the state border with a duck on top of their heads, and Nebraska parents can be arrested if their children burp in church. How fascinating![11]

- A prognosticating website that told me how my name will one day be defined in the dictionary. Apparently, 'Jeff Havens' will one day mean 'a

---

[10] It will probably take you longer to get fired for looking at furniture porn than it will if you look at people porn, and you'll probably just get fired for being weird, but the end result is the same.

[11] But wait, there's more! It's illegal to wear a bulletproof vest while committing a murder in New Jersey. It's also illegal to sing off-key in North Carolina _or_ to use an elephant to plow your cotton fields. Dishes in Oregon must be drip-dried, and Tennesseans cannot shoot anything from a moving car except for whales. Only about 2% of these 'laws' were linked to actual statutes (and who knows if those 'statutes' were real or invented), so it's hard to say how many of them are real...but wait a second! Of course they're real! I found them on the Internet, didn't I?

person with a sixth sense for detecting the presence of goblins.' Or it might mean 'extremely flatulent,' which is the answer I got when I refreshed the page.[12]

- A quiz that provided a picture of a frumpy, disheveled person and then asked whether I thought he or she was a computer programmer or a serial killer. That's thirty minutes of my life I'll never get back. Fun fact, though: some were both!

The above list is the product of a single debauched evening, so imagine the power you'll harness after a couple weeks of eight-hour days spent in such random searching. In no time at all you will be master of the Internet, a fountain of wisdom that will serve you in good stead in your efforts to make interesting small talk while you're standing next to your fellow Internet surfers at the state unemployment office.

Oh! I almost forgot:

When in doubt, go to YouTube.

Where Twitter is the current king of empty social networking, YouTube is the indisputable master of time-wasting in general. If for any reason you find yourself unable to think of a keyword to begin your random searching, simply log on to YouTube and check out what's popular. Any one of those videos will link you to a few more, which will in turn link you to several others,[13] and before you know it you'll be at

---

[12] I'm going with the first one.

[13] In this sense, videos on YouTube employ a transmission and propagation model identical to that of herpes.

the end of day, filled with images of cats playing the piano, teenagers shooting bottle rockets out of their butts, and grown men dipping their nuts in paint thinner. And when it comes to those last two, don't even pretend that you don't want to see them.

Jobhunting on the Job!

Without a doubt, this is one of the brashest, boldest, ballsiest moves you can do. To sit there at your desk, computer on for anybody to see, and surf for better jobs *at the exact moment that you're supposed to be doing the one you're being paid for*, is a tactic so brilliant I am ashamed to admit that I did not come up with it on my own. But please, *please* spend a little a time on this one. You won't regret it.

There are three ways to do this well. One, mentioned above, is to look for a new job while at your current job. Another is to run your own Internet side business – web designer, freelance photographer, pet psychic, online therapist, professional escort, etc. – from your work computer. The kind of business you run doesn't really matter, so long as whatever it is isn't supported in the fine print of your job description. It never hurts to make a few extra bucks on somebody else's dime, especially when those will be the last dollars you make once your infuriated employer discovers what you're doing.

However, since you're trying to get fired, pursuing other jobs at work might seem counterintuitive. If it does, consider the third option: running your very own fantasy league from work. I put this in the 'job' category not because it pays you, but because it can easily suck up forty hours of your life every week. The same is true for any forum you might administer. Interested in connecting with other scrapbooking women from around the world? Curious to see what's current in the European BDSM scene? Then what are you waiting for? Start a chatroom from your office laptop and see what you've been missing!

Pick whichever of these three avenues appeals to you, but understand that any one of them will work with incredible speed. The *second* your boss figures out that you're spending your workday either looking for or actually doing some other job, you'll be unemployed so fast your head will spin.[14]

Make an Attempt at Legitimate Research!

At first this might seem like a misprint. After all, why would you spend time doing real research if your goal is to get fired? But remember, I said 'make an *attempt*' at legitimate research. If you'll remember from the chart at the beginning of this chapter, approximately 0.022% of the Internet is comprised of useful information, while the remainder is made up of lies, slander, conspiracy theories, general inanity, and other forms of misinformation. Thus you can spend your working day online in a sincere effort to perform your job and *still* end up getting fired for putting together a laughably inaccurate report.

Some of you are undoubtedly familiar with this from your college days. I know that most of you, in the process of plagiarizing papers for your class assignments, have cut and

---

[14] Or it would if your leather ball-gag mask didn't prevent your head from moving.

pasted pieces of 'information' that were questionable to say the least. The number of people who have lifted entire passages from Wikipedia articles without bothering to verify the accuracy of that information has been conservatively estimated at 471,000,000,000. So if you've done the same, you're in good company. And in some cases, your professors were either too ignorant or apathetic to notice that your term paper: a) was written in a style that bore no resemblance to your first writing assignments, b) had occasional incoherent moments, almost as though the writer had copied from two separate sources and hadn't bothered to make a decent transition, and c) contained a depth of thought that you had never previously demonstrated and which contrasted wildly with the few short, simple sentences that were the product of your own imagination.

But in other cases, your professors managed to shake themselves out of their depression long enough to take notice of your actions, and what happened? You got an F. Your working experience will be no different.

Now if you're already inclined to plagiarism, chances are you're heading for a career in journalism. Modern journalists are notorious thieves, and they should welcome you into their fold with open arms. For example, Jayson Blair, a reporter for the New York Times, was found in 2003 to have plagiarized several articles and to have invented quotes for a number of other articles. Jack Kelley, a five-time Pulitzer-nominated journalist for USA Today, was forced to resign after investigations revealed a staggering number of instances of plagiarism and fabrication, including – this one's my favorite – writing a story about a woman who perished fleeing

Cuba by boat and then using a picture of a different, *living* woman for the accompanying photograph.

"Well sure," you're probably thinking, "faking stories, quotes, and other information is definitely a great way to get fired. But what's wrong with a little plagiarism? Why should I re-write an idea if I can find exactly what I'm looking for on the Internet?"

I'm glad to hear me ask that question for you, and here's the answer. First, plagiarism is helpful because it means that you really aren't interested in thinking for yourself, which as we've already covered is an excellent way to get fired. But more importantly, plagiarizing blindly from the Internet means that you have somehow maintained the ridiculous belief that the Internet is full of good information. And as long as you keep thinking that, you'll have no problem eventually creating something so monumentally stupid that it someday costs you your job.

All you'll need to do here is spend a little time searching. You're always only a few clicks away from misinformation ranging from theoretically plausible to truly absurd. Here's just a sample of what you might find:

Things I Found on the Internet While Hung Over One Morning

- The rare Northwest tree octopus is facing extinction due to habitat loss and climate change. Fortunately, there is a site designed to raise awareness and, with any good luck, prevent such a tragedy from happening.

- Country superstar Shania Twain is Mark Twain's great-granddaughter.[15]
- According to a handful of websites, the Earth is flat, centered at the North Pole and surrounded by a circle of ice that disbelievers call Antarctica.
- Human brain cells have been transplanted into lab mice with the astonishing result that those mice now exhibit the same level of intelligence as the average human. The site I found also allows you to challenge one of those mice, Clyven, to a cheese maze race, which I'm happy to say I won.
- Customs officials have trained dogs that can distinguish between illegal Cuban cigars and all other cigars.
- The average person eats eight spiders in their sleep every night.[16]
- Aliens have landed on Earth and have interbred with unsuspecting humans to create human-alien hybrids. The site I visited had a picture of NBA point guard Chauncey Billups next to a drawing of a theoretical alien to strengthen the alien-human-

---

[15] Never mind the fact that her real name is Eilleen Regina Edwards, that her 'Twain' comes from her adoptive stepfather, and that in any case Mark Twain's real name is Samuel Clemens, and that *his* 'Twain' comes from steamboat jargon on the Mississippi. Logic has no place here. They're related, which of course is why they look so much alike. I've said it before, and I'll say it again: Mark Twain is a hottie.

[16] Nothing makes a better lie than an assertion that is impossible to disprove. Along those lines, I think you should also know that the average person gains 4.3 pounds every night, which is then off-gassed as serotonin five minutes before waking. Another interesting fact: whales can rhyme.

hybrid claim. If *that* doesn't convince you, I don't know what will.

- The Earth has been conducting natural nuclear fission experiments for hundreds of thousands of years.
- The Holocaust never happened.
- The U.S. government orchestrated the 'terrorist attacks' on the World Trade Center in 2001 and also blew up TWA flight 800 in a missile test.
- Scientists have discovered a way to turn turkey guts into usable crude oil.

There's more, of course, but this should give you a good idea of the potential you have simply in using the Internet for its intended purpose.

Now those of you who have a vested interest in finding decent information online might now be discouraged. After all, if so much crap is out there, how are you supposed to distinguish between legitimate and erroneous information? Are there sources that are considered universally reliable? How can one guarantee that a particular piece of data is sound?

Those are all very good questions, for which I am about to provide you my favorite answer in this book. *Since that isn't the point of this book, I don't care!* I'm here to help you get fired, not to learn how to fact-check the Internet. So do yourself a favor and just assume that everything you read online is accurate. Eventually it will get you exactly where you want to be – sleeping until noon on the inflatable pool toy you call a mattress.

One more thing before we move on: do not overlook the fun you can have by accidentally using the wrong TLD (.com, .org, .gov, etc.) for the website you're attempting to access. Why? Because you can often end up in places you never intended. Years ago, for example, my father wanted to learn something about the White House, so he typed in *www.whitehouse.com*. Only problem is, the official website for the White House is *www.whitehouse.**gov***. At the time, *www.whitehouse.com* was a porn site (it has since been a debt-restructuring site and is now a link to health care reform issues), and my father learned all kinds of human tricks he hadn't known were possible. He tried them. We miss him.[17] But at the time it was hilarious, and it can be fun for you too.

Download *Everything*

And I mean *everything*, people. All the porn, pictures, YouTube videos, Hulu shows, sports clips, job applications, and other crap you accumulate during your weeks of Internet-surfing need to be saved onto your company computer's hard drive.

There are two reasons for this. Number one, your Internet connection at work is almost certainly faster than your connection at home. It might not be as fast as the T1 uber-link you had in college, but it's a lot better than the shared cable or DSL link you're putting up with in your apartment. Take advantage of it while you can.

But more importantly, the reason you need to download everything you can is that, at some point, your

---

[17] Remember, he died in the last chapter.

computer will be used by somebody else. Perhaps a colleague's computer will crash and they'll 'borrow' yours while you're at your four-hour lunch, or perhaps your company's IT department will take your computer over the weekend to do periodic maintenance. And if that person has even a rudimentary sense of curiosity and is willing to spend the fifteen seconds it takes to access your cached downloads...well, let's just say it'll be a special moment when you return to your desk and realize that everyone around you now knows the kind of things you like to look at when you don't think anybody else will find out.

"But What If I Don't Have the Internet at Work?"

Then I'm sorry for you and the depressing job you landed. No Internet? How do you even *live* with yourself? Do you just cry all day long? It's gotta suck.

But if you did manage to snag a 19th-century job, you'll have to do things the old-fashioned way and use the telephone. I know most of you think phones are just for sending text messages, but back in the day their primary function was to allow people to actually speak to each other. In some ways, taking care of personal phone calls at work can be an even better way to waste time than using the Internet, since it will also force your coworkers to listen to all your loud, annoying, inappropriate, non-work-related phone conversations. We're anticipating the Fourth Pillar of Poverty a bit here, but I think you can already appreciate how calling your sister from work to ask about her son's first day in kindergarten is both a great way to waste time *and* irritate a good number of your colleagues.

Well, that's the Internet – and the phone, but mostly the Internet. It's a one-stop shop for destroying your work ethic, and I'm confident that most of you will take to this like ducks to water.

The only problem with using the Internet to get fired – and it is a real problem – is that it often takes a long time before your superiors realize what you're doing. You can go weeks, often months without being detected. You can minimize your search windows or angle the screen away from your doorway; there are definitely ways to waste time online in a clandestine fashion. But don't worry. Eventually you will be found out. Eventually those around you will realize that you're spending your entire day watching YouTube shorts and placing stock trades, and you'll be fired before you know it. I realize that this requires a patience that most of you don't possess, but I'd like you to try anyway. Because if there is one saving grace to the slow build-up of rage that your Internet surfing will cause in those around you, it is that your firing will come swiftly and seemingly out of left field. So if your birthday is in the next few months, get yourself an early present and start surfing now. With any good luck, it'll be wrapped and ready for you to open by the time your special day arrives.

And yet I know that some of you will not be able to successfully destroy your work ethic on your own. You're going to need help, some outside stimulation to really get yourself to the canyon floor of your potential. Fortunately there are a number of well-tested substances that can help you get the job done, and they are the subject of the next chapter. Yes, some of them are illegal, but since when have you let the law get in your way? You didn't stop making consensual love to your high school sweetheart just because the law considered it a statutory crime, did you?

I didn't think so.

Cocaine, Meth, and Other Things to Put in Your Coffee

Time for a break, my diligent readers. In the last five chapters I've asked you to do a lot – actively forge your resume, change the way you dress, spend hours on end surfing the Web – and I know some of you are thinking, "Gosh,[1] I didn't know that getting fired took so much *work*!"

Enter the chapter on substance abuse. The techniques herein should come so easily that it won't feel like you're doing anything at all. Yes, you're going to have to find a way to procure your drug or alcohol of choice, but you've been doing that for a while now and it shouldn't pose any significant problem. And otherwise all you need to do is sit back, relax, pour your favorite poison in, and wait for the world to disappear. And when you wake up – presuming that you do – you should find yourself not only blissfully unemployed but with a big black mark on your employment record that should ensure you never have to suffer the agony of paid work again.

---

[1] Actually, I'm sure that none of you are actually thinking the word 'gosh.' Nobody says that anymore. In fact, 'gosh' was officially retired from the English language in 1993, along with 'grody,' 'gee willikers,' 'henceforth,' and 'Psyche!' with the exclamation point.

Now you'll notice I said drugs _or_ alcohol in the previous paragraph. The truth is, however, that if you're really serious about getting fired, you'll abuse both of them. The ideal student of the **How to Get Fired!** program will experiment with every substance I mention in the next few pages, thus assuring a quick and spectacular professional end.

However, I know that some of you abstain from alcohol for religious reasons, others are afraid of needles and won't try heroin, and still others lack access to the toothless halfwits who brew crystal meth in their kitchen laboratories. So let me put you at ease. You don't have to do everything I'm about to mention. It'd be great if you would, but abusing any one of the following substances will almost certainly cost you your job.

So, are you ready to smoke, snort, drop, pop, drink, and/or inject your way into early retirement? Then read on, my coke-addled minion! Freedom is only a bad trip away!

Alcohol

We'll start with the most popular. Alcohol is the undisputed king of drugs, accounting for approximately $115.9 billion in U.S. sales in 2003. (By comparison, marijuana is thought to bring in around $8.5 billion a year for Mexican drug cartels, who ship most of their products into the U.S., and cocaine a mere $3.9 billion.)[2] According to the Economics Research Service of the United States Department of Agriculture, the average American consumed 21.6 gallons of

---

[2] It's hard to find sales figures for U.S. drug dealers, as most of them don't file taxes.

beer in 2003, an amount that I imagine some of you have knocked out in a weekend of keg parties. Alcohol has a long and illustrious history both in the world and on college campuses. According to a 2002 Harvard University study, 31% of college students abuse alcohol, and 7% are alcoholics. If this describes you, then congratulations! You are well on your way.

Important Tidbit Some of You Will Probably Skip Over #3 – Alcohol, a Brief History

The process of brewing alcoholic beverages has existed for as long as people have wanted to shout obscenities at passersby and have sex without consequences. The first historical evidence of alcohol exists in the form of prehistoric beer mugs dating in some cases back to 10,000 B.C. It is thought that some primitive cultures may have invented beer before inventing bread. For those of you who take a more rigid theological approach to the creation of the world, this means that alcohol was likely invented on the Second Day of Creation, right after light and dark. The Garden of Eden almost certainly had an open bar, which helps explain why it took Adam and Eve so long to figure out that they were naked.

It is not known if there was ever a culture on Earth that did not discover the wonders of alcohol, as those cultures would have been annihilated by their drunken and more warlike neighbors. The Chinese got crunk around 5,000 B.C.; Egyptians were bombed by 4,000 B.C.; India got swishy around

2,700 B.C; Greeks were blitzed around 2,000 B.C.; and Persian chemists perfected Everclear by the 800s A.D. Virtually every kind of food – rice, honey, grapes, potatoes, pineapples, sugar cane, parsley, turnips, ocelots, sand, broccoli – has been fermented to make one form of alcohol or another.

The use of alcohol actually helped improve the health of the ancient world. Because ancient people had no concept of germs or the benefits of rigorous sanitation, they often drank water from contaminated lakes and rivers, which in turn led to various outbreaks of cholera, botulism, typhoid fever, and other ailments. However, because alcoholic beverages require water to be boiled prior to fermentation – a process which has the added benefit of killing any pathogens in that water – many alcoholic drinks were more sanitary than any other available beverage. It is perhaps for this reason that the Mayflower sailed to America with more beer in its holds than drinking water. In fact, the alarming lack of beer by the end of their trans-Atlantic voyage was a major factor why the ship landed at Plymouth Rock instead of continuing on to their intended destination near the Hudson River.

Given that America is a nation founded by raging alcoholics, it makes sense that when a small number of prohibitionists amended the Constitution to outlaw alcohol, the vast majority of the country didn't even pretend to listen. Speakeasies sprang up overnight – by one account, New York City alone had between 30,000 and 100,000 of them – and the black market trade in alcohol led to the precipitous rise of the American Mafia, which until then had contented itself with gambling and thievery. By the end of his tax-evading career, Al Capone controlled virtually all of Chicago's 10,000 speakeasies along with most of the bootlegging trade from Canada to Florida.[3]

Today, alcohol has thankfully resumed its rightful place in the American pantheon – as a staple of accidental pregnancies and traffic accidents everywhere. So drink up, my hearties! I know you're only 19, but your ID says you're 27, and that's good enough for Uncle Sam.

It should come as no surprise that alcohol is the most commonly abused drug in the American workplace. A study by the University of Buffalo's Research Institute on Addictions found that workplace alcohol use affects more than 19 million Americans. For an even more impressive fact, try this one out: the National Institute on Alcohol Abuse estimated that alcohol abuse among American workers led to approximately $185 billion in lost productivity in 1998 dollars. That's like $4 trillion in today's money![4]

So, how can you use all this devil juice to help get you fired? Easy! All you need to do is keep doing what you've

---

[3] And just in case you think it was just gangsters who profited on illegal trading, here's something to consider. Joseph Kennedy, former senator and the father of John F. Kennedy, is said to have increased his fortune through illegal alcohol sales during Prohibition. Those rumors have not been proven, but it seems to fit given the fact that he made his initial fortune by engaging in insider trading on the unregulated stock market of the 1920s. And your parents told you to always play fair...

[4] For a much less impressive fact, a 2006 finding by the National Institute on Alcohol Abuse and Alcoholism concluded that men are more likely to drink on the job than women, and single men are more likely to do so than married men. The fact that they needed to conduct a study to prove this blows my mind. It's like those studies they sometimes do in Britain to prove that sex feels good or that women are fond of shoes.

been doing for the last few years. I know that most of you have been drinking almost continuously since you first arrived on campus. I know that most of you have experienced the magic of a Saturday night blackout. Some of you have engaged in drunken cross-dressing. And don't even pretend that you haven't made out with at least one person whose appearance in broad daylight would repulse you. That's the beauty of alcohol – everybody's gorgeous when you're too drunk to see.

What's more, you've been drinking some of the worst alcohol that has ever been invented, liquid atrocities like Natural Light, Keystone Light (the only beer I've ever had that actually gets *worse* the more you drink it), Clan MacGregor blended scotch/engine cleaner, Mad Dog 20/20, The Beast, and Milwaukee's Best – a name which, if true, only proves that Milwaukee is a sad, sad city. You've gotten drunk on liquor so bad I wouldn't give it to my dog.

Why have you put up with such garbage? Because you've been poor, and that poverty has forced you to economize in ways you no longer have to. Because *you now have a job!* Until you get fired, you have the means to lavish your palate with decent liquor. And if you can knock back a dozen Natty Lights during a single, vigorous game of Beer Pong, imagine how much more you'll be able to drink when your body isn't gagging on the backwash you're feeding it.

But wait, there's more! Because once you've established a pattern of either getting drunk at work or arriving to work hungover – because according to the Harvard School of Public Health, the two essentially amount to the same thing – you'll find that your proficiency plummets. It's hard to stay on top of a deadline when you're clinging to the toilet seat for dear life. So set up a pony keg on the breakroom lunch table, play quarters while you're on the phone with a long-winded customer, pound a couple martinis at lunch, and watch your career wither away!

Prescriptions

For the life of me, I don't know how well-heeled Americans ever survived without prescription drugs. There was a time when obtaining drugs meant buying a greasy bag of heroin cut with flour or strychnine from an equally greasy, unwashed criminal beside a dumpster and a burning trash can – hardly the kind of environment for a respectable member of society. But now, thanks to the proliferation of legal uppers and downers like Ritalin, Adderol, Percocet, Vicodin, and Oxycontin, you can buy drugs from people who won't look askance at you for wearing a tie to the transaction.

As I'm sure most of you already know, prescription drug use has skyrocketed on college campuses, the number of users more than tripling from 1993 to 2005 and the global use of prescription drugs actually exceeding the use of illegal drugs around 2007. The primary reason for this is because most prescription drug abuse starts around eight years old (see inset box). Most people who use prescription drugs do so for one of three reasons: because they've been hooked on uppers since they were teething and would melt if they ever came off of them; to improve their ability to concentrate during long study sessions; or because drinking just isn't as fun without the added twitchiness that only Adderol can provide.

Important Tidbit Some of You Will Probably Skip Over #4 – Ritalin and Adderol, a Briefer History

By even the most conservative estimates, people have been around for several thousand years. People gave birth to baby people, who then forgot to wear condoms and gave birth to new baby people, and so on for a long time. All seemed well.

Then, around 1983 it was discovered that every child on Earth was suffering from one of two terrible disorders – ADD or its caffeinated cousin, ADHD. The human race was suddenly in danger of extinction. But thankfully the same group of scientists who discovered ADD/ADHD immediately formulated a cure for disorders that nobody knew existed until they told us we all had it.

Enter Ritalin and Adderol, the saviors of humanity.

With the introduction of these two drugs, parents everywhere rejoiced. Before, in the dark ages of parenting, young mothers and fathers toiled under the delusion that their screaming, crying, hyper, active, fun-loving children were behaving the way children were supposed to behave. They thought – poor souls! – that a four-year-old who spoke in incomplete sentences and had trouble sitting still was acting, well, like a four-year-old.

In the 1980s, however, parents learned a startling truth: every behavior their children exhibited that had hitherto been considered a natural part of being a child was in fact a symptom of these new sinister, pervasive diseases. More importantly, parents learned that a single pill every morning could shut their kids up long enough for Mom and Dad to enjoy a quiet breakfast. Needless to say, demand for Ritalin and Adderol soared, and some municipalities put it in the water along with fluoride and mercury.

In no time parents everywhere were sprinkling powdered Adderol into their children's cereal, and soon children across the country were displaying the listless, sunken-eyed appearance of drug addicts everywhere. A small number of children seemed to respond favorably to their medication, demonstrating improved test scores and attentiveness in school. But for the most part, kids sank into a slow torpor of insensibility. Parents were overjoyed.

No one really knows what causes ADD/ADHD,[5] but one thing is certain: these disorders will be with us as long as two-year-olds continue to be annoying. I'm just waiting for baby heroin to make it to market. Then we'll _really_ get some peace and quiet.

---

[5] That's a lie. Television and computers cause it, devices whose rapid frame rates so far exceed our normal, evolved experience that our developing brains cannot properly process the speed at which electronic information changes on a screen. The average 30-second commercial changes its focus a few dozen times, while the average 30-second sitting-on-the-floor-of-your-living-room-playing-with-a-Slinky experience changes its focus maybe twice. It's no wonder that toddlers raised on television develop an accelerated expectation for external stimulation which will lead to a subsequent inability to tolerate long, drawn-out activities. Given that our nine-month-old bodies don't yet have the physical dexterity to handle walking, does anybody honestly believe that our nine-month-old brains have the mental dexterity necessary to navigate the lightning world of modern media?

The best thing about abusing prescription drugs – aside from the fact that you can pop pills in plain sight – is the fact that they very rarely kill you. Sure, they killed Heath Ledger and Michael Jackson, and you could develop a potentially fatal tolerance with enough practice. But these drugs come in an orange bottle, which means they're safe to consume.

You'll notice I've focused primarily on Ritalin and Adderol, and I know some of you are saying, "Hey, pal, Adderol's for beginners. I'm a Vicodin man. What about me?" Don't worry, my near-comatose friend. Since Percocet, Vicodin, and Oxycontin are all opiates, we'll be covering their special abilities more thoroughly in the section about heroin. So keep reading – if you can keep your eyes open, that is.

You might also be wondering, "How exactly are these things supposed to help me get fired? After all, I use Adderol to help me study." Well, if you want to get fired, you're going to be popping a *lot* of pills. Having a single Ritalin here or there isn't likely to do too much damage to your career, any more than having a single beer at lunch will lead to your loss of position and salary.

But let's be serious for a moment. Can you remember the last time you took Adderol just for the pleasing rush of it? Just because a pharmacy gave it to you doesn't mean it's not addictive – Oxycontin, for example, is more addictive than heroin. And eventually your ever-increasing tolerance for uppers and painkillers will lead to the inevitable side effects those pills all have. In the case of Ritalin, those side effects include headache, drowsiness, anorexia (perfect for college!), cardiac arrhythmia, erratic changes in blood pressure, Tourette's syndrome (in rare cases, but what a great way to go out with a bang!), hair loss, and nausea. And I've always found that simultaneously throwing up, falling asleep, and shouting random expletives at my coworkers has made it difficult for me to concentrate at work. So wolf 'em down, people!

Plus, starting with legal drugs is a great way to move into the not-so-legal drugs, which it is now time for us to discuss.

Marijuana

I know, I know. Pot is *so* high school. Most of you have already been there and done that, and you've moved on to bigger and better drugs. Plus, you know the truth about marijuana – that it is neither as addictive as alcohol nor as fatal as nicotine. So you might be thinking, "Come on, Grandpa. Pot never killed anybody, and it certainly isn't going to get me fired."

Not so fast, my four-twenty friend. While everything in the previous paragraph is correct, there is an additional truth you need to understand in order to see the advantages of good old-fashioned ganja:

Marijuana is better than any other drug at making its users *lazy as balls.*

In my entire life I have never heard anybody say that marijuana has improved any of their skills or abilities. Sure, you aren't likely to get into a barfight or end the night with a speeding ticket, but you're also not likely to do anything of any value. Don't believe me? Then try on the following test sentences for size.

Sentences You Will Never Hear

1) "Don't worry, he'll be here. He's a huge pothead, he's never late."
2) "These merger and acquisition talks are exhausting. Can anyone pass me the bong?"
3) "This project needs to be taken care of ASAP, and I think the best person for the job is Melanie the Reefer Queen."
4) "I don't mind working through lunch. Just let me roll a fattie and I should be fine."

Enough said.

Cocaine and Heroin

Now we get to the big dogs, two rising stars that will almost certainly get you fired – cocaine, because it makes you incapable of rational thought by ramping you up to a ridiculously high energy level, and heroin because it makes you incapable of pretty much everything. I cannot overemphasize the potential of these two drugs to help you lose work.

But which one to take?

It depends on where you're coming from. If you're already hooked on prescription uppers, then cocaine is the one for you. After all, if you're currently popping three Adderol just to maintain your equilibrium, you're really only a hop, skip, and jump away from snorting blow off a public toilet. Excessive cocaine use can also erode your septum and give you one giant nostril instead of two, which I can guarantee will make you a hit at parties but will also make it impossible for your coworkers to look at you with a straight face.[6] Eventually you'll get fired so your colleagues won't feel embarrassed about mentally judging you, and then huzzah for you! You can start selling your body for angel dust the way you've always wanted.

However, if you're currently a Vicodin, Percocet, or Oxycontin junkie on the order of Rush Limbaugh, then heroin is probably the way you should go. Heroin – otherwise known as dragon, dope, horse, white lady, brown sugar, junk, smack, tar, scat, and about a billion other things – really began its rise to stardom during the Vietnam War, when American soldiers were introduced to it while fighting in the Southeast Asian poppy fields. Heroin was imported in such massive quantities during Vietnam that it's possible the whole 'stop the spread of Communism' thing was just a cover for the war's true purpose of acquiring top-grade heroin at bargain basement prices. And what a drug it is! Without question, heroin is the lowest of the low, the drug you take when you've decided that hope and upward mobility are way overrated. It's also a great choice for those of you who love injecting yourself with a liquid the color of melted butter.[7]

And, as an added bonus, these two drugs will be featured in my next bestselling self-help book, *How to Accidentally Kill Yourself!*, where I will be encouraging my readers to follow in the footsteps of some of America's most

---

[6] I actually know a guy. His nose looks like a vacuum cleaner. It's disgusting, and yet so hypnotic that I can barely stare at anything else. Seriously, it's like a train wreck – you just can't look away.

[7] Full disclosure: writing that sentence – just *writing* it – made me a little queasy.

famous citizens by overdosing on cocaine, heroin, and their derivatives. Here's a taste of what you'll find:

Role Model Time!

- John Belushi of *Animal House* fame overdosed on a speedball (mixture of cocaine and heroin), because one drug just wasn't enough!
- Former major league ballplayer Ken Caminiti, who made a name for himself by being the first major league player to admit using steroids (in his case, during his 1996 MVP season), died from cocaine and assorted opiates!
- Nirvana's frontman Kurt Cobain shot himself in the head with a shotgun after overdosing on heroin – which just goes to show, kids, that sometimes even heroin isn't enough! "Heroin – Shoot Up, Shoot Yourself!"
- Chris Farley, America's funniest fat man, copied John Belushi not only by appearing on Saturday Night Live but also by overdosing at 33 on a speedball!

Hallucinogens

However, if your commitment to getting fired does not include dying, you might want to dabble in the whack-crazy world of psychotropics. These are far less likely to kill you than cocaine or heroin, but they *will* put you in an alternate universe utterly incompatible with getting anything valuable done.

Allow me to set the scene.

Bring Psilocybin to Work Day – Take One

Your alarm kicks you awake at 5:30 am. You have to be at work in 30 minutes, and as usual you don't want to go. You can't bear the thought of another day wasted at work when you could be spending your time doing something, *anything* more enjoyable. You've done your best to grit your teeth and suffer through, but today you just don't think you can handle it. Fortunately, you have a bag of mushrooms and a few tabs of acid lying on the nightstand beside your alarm clock, and you gobble them all down on your way to the shower.

You feel an odd tingling while you're in the shower, which makes perfect sense once you get out and look at yourself in the mirror. You've sprouted horns. You try to comb around them, which is difficult because your elbows are bending the wrong way and the horns keep moving – stupid horns! But they're kind of cool, too, and once they start talking you find yourself unable to stop laughing. Those horns are hilarious!

Time to get dressed. All the clothes in your closet are made out of granola bars, which sounds great because you're *starving*. You eat a couple sleeves, tell the dwarf hiding in your sandals to keep an eye on things while you're gone, and settle into your pigeon on your way to work. Yesterday it was a car – today, it's a pigeon. Don't forget to buckle up!

Traffic is unbearable this morning because all the roads are made of gravy. Too bad you can't just fly...but wait a minute...wait just a minute...yes you can! You engage your pigeon's flight button, and you're off, soaring well above the gravy roads and pancake boats and sparkly jumjawobs – what the hell is a jumjawob? – that drift below you like ants on a pickle. The setting moon is an oyster, and the rising sun smells like bacon.

This is the best Wednesday *ever*.

Your pigeon settles in gracefully beside a row of red and green and swirly ostriches, and you slide into work. 'Walk' isn't really the right term for it, because you've misplaced all your bones. Maybe they're in your pigeon's butt. You'll have to check the butt when you leave.

All right, you made it. Time to finally conquer the Troll King once and for all. Your first stop is the bathroom, of course, because that's where you keep your sword. You spend fifty-three minutes washing your hands, because the water is going *inside* of you, and the feeling of being filled like a balloon is too exquisite to pass up. You'd have kept going, too, but the sink got angry and turned into a thorny lizard, and it wouldn't give you the taco. Stupid lizard sink!

You're not actually sure how you make it to your desk – maybe it came to you – but once you're there you attach yourself to your seat. Literally, your seat stitches itself to you, and you spend half an hour trying to extricate yourself. The walls of your cubicle have teeth now, orange teeth made out of pointy baby dinosaurs, and to get away from them you crawl under your desk, chair and all, and hope that the floor stops rippling.

At this point you're interrupted by the fleeting thought that maybe those mushrooms were cut with something unholy, but you don't have time to dwell on it. It's raining under your desk now, and you're terrified of drowning. Where's a velvet lifejacket when you need one?

I could go on if I wanted to and tell you about how I ended up on the floor of my local prison, sucking on concrete and praying for my tail to go away, but I think I've made myself clear. Hallucinogens are fine if you want to fit in at Bonnaroo, but they're not so good for working. So load up on PCP, my squirrel-faced friend, and watch your career fade away!

Crystal Meth

Wow.

That's pretty much all I can say about this one. You know how I said heroin was the lowest of the low? Well, I was lying. I wrote that part before I learned what the ingredients in crystal meth are, and man! Let me tell you, I cannot *wait* to get my hands on some of this stuff.

Crystal meth is becoming increasingly popular on college campuses and is comprised of ingredients that have absolutely no business being inside the human body. The exact composition of a given batch varies from mixture to mixture, but some of the better concoctions include:

I Can't Believe I'm Not Making Any of These Up

- Sodium hydroxide (aka lye,)[8] an industrial cleaner used in metal etching and also by municipal workers who occasionally dispose of roadkill by dissolving the bodies in lye solutions
- Anhydrous ammonia, used most commonly in fertilizer and refrigerants
- Match tips
- Drano
- Brake fluid
- Lighter fluid
- Hydrochloric acid, which will literally eat away human flesh

The fact that somebody ever said, "Hey, what if we added brake fluid, anybody up for giving that a shot?" blows my freaking mind. But somebody did, and now meth is a drug that simultaneously offers a longer high than cocaine and tends to be even more fatal.

But the real secret to meth's ability to get you fired is in one of its side effects. Yes, it kills your sex drive, drastically increases your chance of heart attack and stroke, and slowly dissolves your brain, but those things won't get you fired. The one that will, though, is a condition known as 'meth mouth,' the most telltale sign of meth addiction and one that generally makes your mouth look like an open sewer. I've seen pictures, people – it's *disgusting*, rows of missing and cracked and

---

[8] You know, that thing Brad Pitt poured on Ed Norton's hand in *Fight Club* to permanently scar it? Mmm, I want it inside me.

rotten teeth staring back at you like half-decayed cadavers. Trust me, there's not an employer in the world who wants a person with meth mouth to be anywhere near their customers. Nothing says, "Fire me!" quite like employees who look as though they've been run through an industrial dryer. Which leads us to a general rule of employment:

If the first word people use to describe you is 'haggard', you're going to be fired soon.

Perhaps you think I've gone too far. After all, meth and crack are just about the lowest drugs you can take, so what employee in their right mind would do them?

Tons of people! In 2004, 129,079 people were _treated_ for meth addiction, to say nothing of the untold numbers who didn't bother seeking help. And I can guarantee you, folks, not all of them were living off welfare. Some of them held steady, paying jobs.

So juice up, my toothless friends – opportunity awaits!

Make Your Own!

For those of you who are entrepreneurially minded, you might be thinking, "If clinical idiots can make a popular drug out of matches and brake fluid, surely I can do the same with axle grease and spent uranium." And the answer is – absolutely! If you're tired of paying for your drugs, or if you just like to mix chemicals and see what explodes, making your own is the way to go.

If you choose this option, remember this: _If it's toxic or corrosive, it probably confers a wicked high._ Thus, the substances you should be considering can most easily be obtained in the cleaning section of your local grocery store or in those skull-and-crossbones trucks you see on the highway. Liquid nitrogen, anthrax, C-4, the blood from the alien in *Alien* – any of these would be a great place to start.

But whether you make your own drugs or inhale the ones already available, drug use is a remarkably easy way to get fired. As far back as the 1970s it was estimated that one in every forty U.S. employees was using drugs at work, and by 2005 drug addicts were thought to account for a majority of the almost $50 billion in stolen tools, supplies, and office machinery every year.[9] In 2005, drug users were considered three times more likely to have a work-related accident and ten times more likely to take sick days than their sober colleagues. And if times get tight, who are you likely to let go – the guy who shows up on time every day, or the one who calls in sick all the time because withdrawal has made him too jittery to properly operate his car?

But more to the point, habitual drug users are notoriously good at hiding their addictions in the short-term and notoriously bad at doing so in the long-term. And while your boss might excuse a few days of poor performance due to lack of sleep, lingering illness, stress, or any of the other excuses you offer, eventually he or she will start to see more than weariness in your jaundice-colored eyes.

---

[9] Stealing from work, by the way, is another great way to get fired. I know a guy who once got fired for using a company-issued credit card for almost $30,000 of personal purchases. Now of course you don't have to be a drug addict to get fired for stealing; the guy I'm talking about wasn't. But imagine how much *more* he would have stolen if he'd needed the cash to score some crank!

And then, congratulations!   You'll be out the door before you know it, free as a bird to break into your neighbor's houses for things to pawn.

So there you have it. I think we've done an excellent job of destroying your work ethic. We've now covered _when_ to go to work, _how_ to go to work, and how to _do_ your work. But now we need to shift our focus a little and discuss how to act around your colleagues, how to make them despise you so much that it eventually costs you your job. In short, you need to know how to be an *******.[10]

And I know exactly what you need to do. So turn the page, eager reader! Drink in the glory of the picture that follows, and then keep reading to learn how you can ultimately make yourself so loathsome and unwelcome that your coworkers will soon be _begging_ to help you lose your job.

---

[10] How do you like _that_, censor people! The asterisks mean that I didn't curse! Huzzah for asterisks and completely illogical decency laws, but mostly for asterisks! I ******* love them!

Flaunt Your Intolerance

We've come at last to the fourth and final Pillar of Poverty, alienating your coworkers. Now I know some of you are nervous about this section. You've met your fair share of intolerable people, and you're probably thinking, "They are so *good* at it. It's almost as if their caustic personality and deplorable interpersonal skills are genetic, and I don't know if I have it in me."

Relax. I'm sure you're a much worse person than you think you are, and you've spent your life attempting to suppress the dark urges that are always so close to turning you into a raving sociopath. All I'm going to do is help you coax those facets of yourself to the surface.

In fact, there are so many ways to do this that it's hard to know where to begin. So let's start with an easy one. The first step toward alienating your co-workers – and in many ways, the most enjoyable one – is to flaunt your intolerance. By projecting a sense of your superiority over everyone around you, you should very quickly create a working environment as toxic and unhealthy as the supposedly 'fresh' water of the Chicago River.

So pay attention. Because if there's only one piece of advice to gain from this chapter, it's this:

You are better than everyone around you, and you need to make that clear at every opportunity.

Impose Your Moral Superiority

Let's face it – everybody is better than everybody else. I'm so much better than you that it's not even funny. I'm a better writer, scholar, lover, friend, musician, pastry chef, carnival barker, jellyfish tamer, mime, political theorist, horticulturist, mammal – *everything*. I'm pretty much the pinnacle of human evolution. And I'm sure deep down you think the same thing about yourself.

Hearken back if you will – hearken, I say – to your college experience. If you joined a fraternity or sorority then yours was the best on campus, and the people who didn't rush were pathetic and poorly dressed. If you didn't go Greek it's because the people who did were shallow *untermenschen* hardly worth saving from a burning building, much less talking to. If a girl wouldn't give you the time of day, it's because she's a vapid bimbo who's only pretty as long as she never says anything. If your professors delighted in handing out bad grades, it's because they're miserable wretches whose only sadistic pleasure on this planet is to bring others down to their level. And if the person driving in front of you isn't going at least as fast as you are…well, you know the answer to that one.

Raising ourselves up at other people's expense is part of the human condition. Groups of people have always disapproved of other groups of people, and it's something that we Americans take special pride in. After all, we live in the greatest country in the history of ever, a self-evident truth which we have never gotten tired of telling ourselves.[1] So if you want to stay in this country, you need to start openly admitting that you're better than everyone around you. You've been thinking it for years – now's the time to act on it.

So how can you make the jump from thought to action? The best way is to just start telling everybody how great you are and – more to the point when it comes to getting fired – how sorry and weak everyone around you is. But if you can't bring yourself to do this right away, there is a very simple five-step program to help you develop an ability to deride everyone you come in contact with.

Five Steps to a More Condescending You

- Watch *The Bachelor* or *The Bachelorette*.
- Watch *Flavor of Love, Rock of Love*, or any show that ends in '*Of Love.*'
- Watch *America's Got Talent* or *American Idol* (particularly the outtakes)
- Watch *Last Comic Standing*
- If any of these are off the air by the time you're reading this book, watch any reality show.

Reality television is categorically the best method for developing your sense of moral superiority that has ever been invented. It took a few decades, but television producers have finally realized that Americans are dying for opportunities to feel better about themselves by trashing the people they're

---

[1] True, we don't have the highest median income, the healthiest population, the longest life expectancy, the most highly educated public, or the happiest citizenry, but we are still number one! Number one, baby! And anybody who says otherwise is a communist.

watching on television, which of course is why the only shows that *aren't* reality shows anymore can only be found on the Oxygen Network and Univision.

This method is so easy it should be illegal. The second you sit down to watch an episode of *The Bachelor* with your friends, you'll find yourself compelled to make derogatory comments about one of the contestant's clothes, laugh, walk, manner of speech, or attitude. You'll delight in seeing *America's Got Talent* hopefuls embarrass themselves in front of millions because they were dumb enough to think that dog-juggling is a talent America is eager to see more of. And a few minutes of *Last Comic Standing* will convince you that you're destined for comedy greatness yourself; after all, these people made it on, and most of them suck![2]

By the end of a full season of your reality show of choice, you'll find yourself automatically judging everything about everybody you see on television, and most importantly you'll be doing it *out loud*. And once you're used to saying

---

[2] Most of them actually *do* suck, and here's why: that show is rigged. You know those scenes with lines of hopefuls bending around the side of the comedy club? They cut those lines off about ten people past the corner – all they want is that camera shot. The *only* people who get on that show are people who have connections to the producers of the show, which is why you'll watch the final 12 and wonder to yourself, "Half of these people are truly awful, are they really the best 12 out of the 10,000 applicants?" Nowhere close, but they know the right people. At least *American Idol* has the decency to make sure that *its* final twelve can sing better than your average shower crooner. Everybody in comedy knows that *Last Comic Standing* is rigged, and if letting you in on the secret makes you less inclined to watch the show, I'll feel like I've done my job. That show has put so many unfunny people in front of the nation that it's lowered the national opinion of comedy as an art form. That being said, if anybody offers me a chance to get on the show, I'll take it – it is, alas, the only game in town. But after this paragraph, I think my chances are slim. ☺

condescending and mean-spirited things to your television, it's only a flop, trip, and jiggle away from doing the same thing in the office.

Here's an example. Remember how I encouraged you to drench yourself in perfume? Well, Sally over in Accounts Payable doesn't wear any at all, and she smells like a warthog. And what's with Bob's new haircut, and those pants! He looks like he should be handing out towels at a retirement center swimming pool. And did you *see* this report that Suzanna just sent out? I don't know what University of Phoenix knockoff she 'attended' to get her 'degree' (do the air quotes), but the woman is barely literate. Still, I'll take her over Steven any day. Anybody with a beard that thick has got to be hiding something.

I could go on – and in my head, I am – but I think you can see how adopting a reality-show mentality in the workplace can help you separate yourself from the Cro-Magnon oafs you're forced to share an office with.

But what if you don't like reality television? What if you, like me, think it's a shallow and degrading waste of time?

Then congratulations! You're already used to feeling superior to others. You already know that you're better than all those TV junkie Morlocks with their empty marriages and meaningless lives. Give yourself a haughty golf clap – you've learned this lesson all on your own!

Don't Forget Religious Superiority!

This one's a no-brainer, and I mean that literally. Given that there are dozens of different religions and thousands of ways to worship within each of those religions, and further given that most religions preach love and tolerance as part of their core beliefs, you would literally have to be without a brain to argue that your religion is superior to that of your co-workers.

And yet people do this all the time. Claiming divine favor is a great way to irritate just about everyone you know. Because nothing can aggravate your colleagues quite like telling them that they're all going to hell.

To do this properly, let everyone know how much you disapprove of the way they're living, and make sure they know you disapprove because they're living in a manner contrary to the teachings of your faith. It doesn't matter if you know the first thing about them, although we will cover the exploitation of other people's personal lives more thoroughly in *Gossip 101*. What matters is that they don't think exactly the way you do. Nobody does, not even the people who worship right beside you every week. Which is why you can use this technique on everyone.

So what can you say to let them know how fallen they are? Well, I know you may not be Christian, but I'm going to use a Christian example because you'll all be familiar with it and it aptly illustrates my point. A lot of people are fond of saying *What Would Jesus Do?*, and it's a very good choice – brief and subtle, with just the right amount of passive-aggressive judgment thrown in. But if you really want to get fired quickly, you'll change this very slightly and say instead:

That's Not How Jesus Would Do It!

The more prescriptive and intolerant you are, the faster you'll be able to claim unemployment. And if anyone retaliates by suggesting that you should be more culturally sensitive or religiously tolerant, don't be afraid to call them a heretic. Trust me, that'll shut 'em up nice and quick.

And if you want to knock this one out of the park, you'll invent your own religion. Why? Because people are inherently comfortable with established religions and inherently uncomfortable with new ones. So while you might annoy your co-workers by preaching the Gospels in the breakroom, it's not likely to get you fired, especially since some of co-workers will support your dedication to the Christian faith.

However, if you come into work on Monday and start preaching the glories of Udu, the Holy Gopher...

Wise and Benevolent Udu, the Holy Gopher
flanked by Ashtaroth and Fluffytime, Udu's Unicorn Disciples, and the Songbirds of the Apocalypse

...you'll get noticed a lot more quickly.

To facilitate your religious awakening, carry a stick with you at all times and constantly refer to it as your 'wand' or 'talisman.' Wear mismatched clothes – purples and lime greens are always good choices – and walk around as though you're seeing things others cannot. Practice staring without blinking, and do so until the force of your gaze causes your coworkers to turn away in discomfort. Then, in an ominous tone, say the following:

"Udu does not approve of the way you're living your life. He is a wise god, loving and merciful, benevolent and forgiving. But he can be wrathful as well."

Udu's reaction to disbelievers and the cities they live in

"And if you do not turn from your sinful ways and walk in His divine footsteps, you will spend eternity roasting in his fiery belly!"

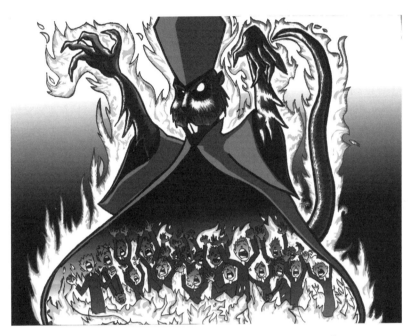

Stuffed with the souls of the damned

(Six seconds of blinkless staring.)
"Is that what you want?"

And rest assured, my friend, you will be fired in no time.

Denigrate the Accomplishments of Others!

But there are two halves to intolerance. The first, which I think we've now covered very effectively, involves creating an unreasonably high opinion of yourself with respect to others. The flip side of that coin, however – and the secret to true arrogance – is to divorce everyone else's accomplishments from anything that could be construed as talent, skill, merit, ability, intelligence, dedication, hard work, or any other desirable quality. If you didn't do it yourself, then by Udu, it's not worth doing!

How do you do this? Simple – by making up reasons why this or that accomplishment isn't really as good as other people seem to think. By now your reality-show mentality should be perfected to the point where you can find faults where none actually exist, and this will be crucial in depicting yourself not only as a self-absorbed megalomaniac but also as someone who has no respect whatsoever for anybody around you.

The best time to practice this technique is when somebody other than yourself gets promoted. Now this might seem counter-intuitive, since you'd rather get fired than promoted. But just because you're on your way out doesn't mean you want to see anybody moving up – *especially* not people who are beneath you in every possible way. So it will be important to explain those promotions in negative terms. A few examples should illustrate this point nicely.

Things Some People Actually Have the Guts to Say – And So Should You!

1) "Yeah, Betty, congrats on that executive directorship. They had to put a woman in there someday, didn't they? Right place, right time, huh. Good for you."

2) "You know the only reason they made Andrew assistant manager is because his aunt used to date the boss. I mean seriously, Andrew's got as much managerial potential as my colon."

3) "I tell you what, if I was just one-sixteenth Cherokee I'd be running this place. Worked for Alex, didn't it?"

I call this particular technique "Office Racist" – not so much because everything you'll be saying is tied to race, but because you'll be framing everyone else's accomplishments as the result of gender, nepotism, race, religion, and other completely arbitrary conditions.

Can it get you fired? Absolutely! In some cases it can have you out the door by the end of the week. But at the very least it will paint you as a bitter and intolerant person, jealous of all and gracious to none, and eventually your unhealthy effect on your workplace will lead you exactly where you're trying to go.

Interestingly, this technique will be easier if you paid attention to the lessons in *The Not-Quite-Eight Habits of Highly Defective People*. Why? Because in general, everyone on the planet is afraid of someday being discovered as a fraud. In a part of your brain you don't like to acknowledge, you're waiting for the day when the whole world tells you that you're not as attractive, intelligent, or competent as you've been allowed to believe. In most cases, this fear is more fear than truth. However, if you're genuinely incompetent *and aware of it*, you will have a much easier time seeing other people's accomplishments (promotions, bonuses, etc.) as an implicit attack on your deficiencies. It probably isn't – let's face it, you're not the center of everyone's universe – but what's important is that you view anybody else's victory as your own defeat.

Now I know some of you have been given this book as a joke by people who thought you might enjoy it – as though the words 'enjoy' and 'reading' could possibly belong in the same sentence – and you've been perusing these pages despite the fact that you secretly want to stay gainfully employed. At this point, I imagine some of you are thinking, "But what if somebody in my office actually *did* get promoted for ancillary reasons such as gender, race, or other unimportant factors? Aren't I honor-bound to rail against such practices?"

And to that I say, congratulations. You've done something I had barely hoped to dream for – you've managed to make your arrogance seem innocent. The very notion that you alone, of all the people in the world, have managed to achieve your current level of proficiency without anyone else's help is a feat of selective intelligence that I truly did not think you had the capacity for. Not to mention that the very thought of crediting someone's success to their race or gender implies that you know everything there is to know about that person's inner qualities, a flat impossibility you have nevertheless chosen to ignore. Who are you to say that, all things being equal, the black applicant will be hired over the white applicant solely based on his or her race – and furthermore, in what magically ideal world could two candidates for a given position possibly be equal in all respects but race? And yet you're thinking it anyway! Congratulations again!

Hopefully this chapter has helped reinforce the central tenet of the Third Pillar of Poverty – namely, that not everything you can do to get fired will require you to learn a new skill. Unless you are unlike anyone I've ever met, you already have within you the seeds of intolerance that, if properly nurtured, will help you become as odious and loathsome to others as your soon-to-be-ex job is to you.

But it's one thing to be intolerant. It's another thing entirely to expand that intolerance into the realm of lies, slanders, and exaggerations that will make you the bane of everyone else's existence. So do some sit-ups, pound down some electrolytes, and do whatever else you usually do to get those creative juices flowing, people. It's time to gossip!

Gossip 101

Did you hear? Well, I'm not really supposed to be telling you this, but, uh – you can keep a secret, right? OK, well ap*par*ently – and this is just what I heard, OK, so don't quote me on it or anything – but ap*par*ently Denise? You know Denise, right, she's over in claims – and she's on her third marriage, by the way, which should tell you a little about *her* people skills – anyway, so I was sitting in the breakroom, having coffee, minding my own business – you know me, I'm not one to pry – but I'm just sitting there and in walks Tim and Gerald. And I don't usually like talking to Tim, because his voice! My God, it's like nails on a chalkboard, I wonder if he got in a bicycle accident as a kid or something. Anyway, so Tim says, 'Did you hear about Denise?' And I was like, 'No, what about her?' So *he* says…

Oh, gossip, you saucy mistress you. From time immemorial, engaging in baseless gossip has been one of the best methods ever devised to make others detest you. It's one thing for your enemies to gun you down in broad daylight, or face you in single combat with a sword and a too-revealing leather thong – at least then you have a chance to defend yourself. But gossip is a ninja, attacking from the shadows and retreating before you can retaliate. It's one of the most devilish weapons ever created, and it is definitely one you'll want to include in your toolkit of ways to get yourself fired.

But before we go into depth on how to use gossip to destroy all of your personal and professional relationships, let's take a walk down memory lane, shall we?

Nostalgic Moment #3

Recess, fifth grade. Location: the blacktop behind your school. Some of your classmates are playing kickball, others Four Square, and still others are searing their own flesh by sliding down the 400-degree metal slide in too-short shorts. Boogers are flying in every direction.

This is where the gossip begins.

In ragged collections of twos and threes, the word makes its way around the playground like cold sores at a trade show in Vegas. Yesterday, Billy saw Becky and John making out behind the third-grade wing; Billy's pretty sure he saw John's hand _under Becky's shirt!_ A scandalized and indignant Becky has denied the rumor for days, which of course means it's true. Beside you, Nick calls Becky a slut. You don't know what that means exactly, but you're pretty sure Becky is one, and at any rate you agree so you won't look stupid.

But wait, there's more! Tyler's parents are getting divorced, and Nick is pretty sure that it's because Tyler's a gaywad – not just gay, but an entire _wad_ of it. Plus, Jill told Kyle at lunch that she won't go out with him, which is definitely going to be weird since Jill and Kyle's sister are best friends. Nathan says he broke his arm in a skiing accident, but Alex is pretty sure it's because his parents beat him. And Harold, who is going to have to wait another fifty years to fully grow into his name, says he saw Tanner smoking a cigarette! And Nick corroborates it!

It's all too much for you. Your head is spinning, reeling from all the intrigue. Fortunately Nick, who seems to have a firmer grasp on the political scene than you do, promises to pass you a super-secret note after recess – triangle-folded no less, the fifth-grade equivalent of a retinal scan – so you can digest it all. You thank him and head toward the dodgeball game to sub in for one of the dozen or so kids who just got pelted in the face and are now bawling hysterically.

But just before you're out of earshot you hear Nick say something to the rest of the group, something that makes everybody laugh. You turn and ask if it was about you. Nick swears it wasn't, but everyone else is still smiling a little too much, and you don't believe him. Maybe Nick isn't as benevolent as he seems.

Maybe, just maybe, it's time to tell the world that Nick's father is an alcoholic.

If you're honest with yourself, you'll admit that elementary school is where you first learned to hate other people, and that hatred has only grown over the years. Those of you who have lived in campus housing or any other tightly-knit community already know how a single rumor can poison the dynamic of an entire group. Moreover, gossip works like nuclear waste in the sense that you don't need much of it to cause massive problems. Indeed, gossip has led to some atrocious consequences – part of the reason the Japanese fought so tenaciously against Allied troops at the end of

World War II is because the citizens were told that the invading Americans would eat their children[1] – but for our purposes we're going to focus less on violence and more on disharmony.

So sit back and enjoy! Because the rules that govern gossip haven't changed much since your elementary school days. You might be older and less adorable than you were fifteen or twenty years ago, but I know the little boy or girl inside of you is still alive and well. So go get 'em, tiger – gootchy gootchy goo!

Exploit the Weakness of Others!

For those of you who ever punched a friend or sibling for absolutely no reason whatsoever, this section should read like an ice cream sundae – in a word, scrumptious. Exploiting the failings of other people is the first step in creating truly awe-inspiring gossip. But in this case, the major weakness you'll be manipulating is mental rather than physical.

So, what is this mental defect? Namely, that people *trust you*. Everyone enters this world with a full tank of trust, and most of us do everything we can to keep it as full as possible. And so, idiots that we are, most of us will give you the benefit of the doubt with almost everything you say. After all, what possible motivation do you have to lie? In most cases a person will have to catch you in a lie several times before he or she stops believing you – and even then, in the back of their heads they'll wonder if maybe next time will be different. This gullibility – I mean, trust – is the reason that Britain and

---

[1] Once again, I'm not making this up.

France continued to appease Hitler long after he had revealed himself to be a pathological liar, and it is the same reason you will be able to poison your workplace with malicious rumors as soon as you get comfortable enough to do so.

Make no mistake, my future pariah – trust will be the downfall of your coworkers. As long as they trust you, you have power over them. Because if there's one thing I've learned from the movies, it's this: if I am ever part of an evil crime syndicate, I'll need to kill everyone else in it before they try to kill me. If I trust my evil crime syndicate partners to take care of me once I've outlived my usefulness to them, I'll end up buried in concrete faster than you can say Jimmy Hoffa.

Begin with the Truth!

"The truth?" you might be thinking. "That doesn't make any sense. What does truth have to do with gossip?"

Nothing. The wonderful thing about gossip, as most of you already know, is that it doesn't have to be true, and we'll cover that in the next section. But I've always found that a great way to wean your way into a gossipy mentality is to share facts about other people's lives. It's easy to do – after all, you're used to talking about the various things that you observe in a given day – and you'll quickly realize that talking about other people gives you the same rush you get from prescription uppers, which you should be thoroughly addicted to by now if you've been paying any attention at all.

I recommend beginning with the innocuous, something like, "Hey Sue, did you see John's sunburn? Looks like he gave himself the second-degree – ouch!" This will get you in the habit of talking about other people's eccentricities and flaws. Plus, it's an uncontestable fact. If Sue argues the point, you can always walk her over to John's office and show her his peeling nose and tomato-orange face as proof of your honesty. She'll leave chastened, and you can add her to the list of people you'll start gossiping about once you work your way up to full-blown lying.

This kind of gossip is almost always benign – so-and-so got a new car, a new suit, a promotion, etc. – and it typically falls into the realm of polite office talk. These topics are safe and usually generic, without the opportunity for judgment that is the hallmark of the truly skilled gossiper. Put simply, telling your coworkers about somebody's new haircut is not going to get you fired. But it *is* going to establish you as a person who knows what's going on around the office, the person others can come to if they want to be up-to-date on everyone else's lives. The key here is for you to be quick on the draw; you want to be the *first* person in the office to notice everything about everybody else. Notice, then tell others – that's the M.O. of the good gossip. Before you know it you'll find yourself in a position of modest authority, an authority that you should waste no time in abusing.

So how do you use this skill to lose your job?

Well, you'll first need to branch into more divisive subjects – divorces, affairs, run-ins with the law, and so forth. Again, stick with the truth for a while. By now you should have mastered the innocent comment, but now you want to start putting some mild judgment into things. Attach caveats to all of your sentences, which is the simplest (and most common) way to mask your judgment of others.

Ways to Pretend That You're Not Being Self-Righteous

- "I don't want to come across callous or anything, but..."
- "Now I'm normally the last person to tell anybody else how to live their life, but..."
- "I'm not one to judge, but..."
- "Is it just me, or..."
- "I know I'm not perfect. I do. But..."

This should be easy, since everybody judges everybody else, and most of us tend to think that we come out on top.[2] So your coworkers should be more than happy to add their own mild judgment to whatever topic you've given them.

And they will stay on your side until, of course, you turn on them.

If you do this right, you'll soon find yourself offering value judgments on all your coworkers without actually seeming to. Gradually your inoffensive 'small talk' gossip will metamorphose into something more devious, much as a fuzzy lion cub eventually grows into a ravening mankiller. But as long as the things you're talking about retain a kernel of truth, several of your coworkers will be happy to play along, and you'll find yourself able to offer more and more severe judgments without reproach.

This process can play out for a long time and will undoubtedly give you another way to waste time that would otherwise be spent on boring, meaningless work. But

---

[2] I haven't yet met the person who's willing to say, "Yeah, I'm pretty much the bottom of the bell curve." But I know he or she is out there.

eventually you'll come to realize a truth that so many recently-fired people already know: it's not just this or that colleague upon whom you should pass judgment. It's *everybody*. Everyone you work with has at least one flaw – bad breath, bad credit, bad dye job, bad marriage – that the rest of the world needs to know about.   And you need to be the spokesperson for that flaw.

And if you can't think of anything. If something does not readily present itself, then you need to make something up. Because at its best, gossip isn't about the truth at all. It's about entertaining lies.

Say Goodbye to Rationality!

The best gossip is simultaneously untrue and unrelated to anything resembling logic.   You'll want to begin your campaign of office terror by studying some of the masters who have come before you, professional hatemongers such as Ann Coulter, Sean Hannity, Al Franken, and Bill Maher.   When these people make their various claims, they're not bothered by such trivialities as coherence and reasoned analysis. On the contrary! When Ann Coulter railed against John Edwards, it wasn't because he was an empty politician who never took a definitive stance on any contentious issue; it was because he had a gay haircut. When Bill Maher blasted George W. Bush, it wasn't because he was criminally shortsighted in his prosecution of the Iraq War; it was because he was from Texas and talked funny. These people have learned that as long as you talk loudly enough, quieter people will lend a credible ear.

How do they do it? Because they've mastered the two primary methods of spreading unfounded rumors: the *ad hominem* argument and my personal favorite, the *non sequitur*. *Ad hominem* attacks aim to insult a man or woman's personal qualities without bothering to address that person's ideas (e.g. Ann Coulter's "John Edwards would be a bad president because he has a fairy haircut."), and *non sequiturs* are pairs of ideas that have absolutely nothing to do with one another. The next time you hear Lou Dobbs argue that the problem with health care is the fact that illegal immigrants are stealing our jobs, you'll know exactly what I'm talking about.

Now I don't expect you to be as proficient at this as Glenn Beck, who has been known to formulate his opinions by using a random word generator. But when you invent stories about your coworkers, you'll want to be both sensational and ludicrous. The crazier your claims are, the less likely people will contest them – because once again, why would you lie?

So, if you've returned from the holidays[3] and you notice that one of your compatriots has lost a little weight, it is safe to begin spreading the rumor that he or she is a leper. (A lot of people will go for the obvious 'bulimia' claim here, but that one's been overdone.) If he or she has gained a few pounds, then it should be clear that they have been possessed by the devil.

To help you get started, I've included a sampling of the kinds of rumors you can begin in your office. A lot of these are already common in offices around America, so once you start using them you should find yourself in good company.

---

[3] Hopefully *all* of them; re-read the *Work – To Go or Not To Go* section of **Treat Your Job Like College** if you need a refresher.

Ideas for Inventing Gossip

Condition	Possible Rumors
Keeps to him/herself	Sleeps with animals 'Person of interest' in area murder Involved in a fight club
New to town	Witness protection Alien scout sent to study Earth Mentally unstable
Unusually happy	Addicted to anti-depressants Embezzling from company Only six months left to live
Recently promoted	Sleeping with the boss Involved in a discrimination lawsuit Keeps kids in cages
Unmarried	Impotent Fond of odd fetish Emotionally crippled
Nice to everybody	Has a few too many cats Received electroshock therapy Engages in self-mutilation

The possibilities are only limited by your creativity. So go wild! As soon as you make the transition from factual to invented gossip, you'll find that there are not enough hours in the day to create elaborate, slanderous lies about the people unfortunate enough to be forced to work in the same building with you.

Important Tidbit Some of You Will Probably Skip Over #5 – Killer Gossip, Literally!

I know that the purpose of this book is to help you get fired, but I feel like I would be remiss if I didn't mention at least one additional benefit to using gossip in your everyday life: namely, as a great way to get rid of people who either annoy you or have things that you want. Some people just won't take a hint, and others stubbornly remain where they are no matter how reprehensible a neighbor you make yourself. And when that happens, gossip can be a great way to take them out of the picture – forever.

Some of the best examples of killer gossip are the whispering campaigns that have invariably accompanied every political, social, and religious purge. The purge is a permanent fixture of the human landscape and has been used by every culture civilized enough to hate another group of people. The purges of Marius and Sulla in pre-imperial Rome, Robespierre's Reign of Terror, the Russian pogroms of 1881-1905, the Khmer Rouge – all of these involved the killing of innocent people, and none of them would have been nearly as destructive without neighbors 'informing' on one another. Once a government has declared a certain kind of person an enemy of the state, all you need to do is mention that so-and-so happens to fall into that undesirable category, and voila! Their hastily vacated house and land are yours! Imagine the joy you'll experience sipping tea on your new patio while your former neighbors flee in terror from the approaching Gestapo! There are few pleasures quite like it.

Perhaps the most famous American examples of killer gossip are the Salem witch trials of 1692-1693, which led to the execution of twenty people and the death in prison of thirteen others. These trials are especially noteworthy because gossip was the _only_ reason for anyone's conviction. In most purges, gossip merely exaggerates a pre-existing dysfunction – a government decides it doesn't like Bolsheviks, or socialists, or foreigners, and you let the authorities know that your neighbor just so happens to be one – but in Salem, there was no active search for witches until a few people started whispering about the weird lady down the street, and boom! Death by hanging. How do you know they're a witch? Because I said so, that's how! You can't argue with that logic, can you?

Someday we'll all find out for certain whether there's an afterlife, and if there is then I suspect a lot of these gossipy types will be spending a decent portion of eternity being burned with hot irons. But until then, enjoy what you can! There's no reason to deny yourself a few acres of your neighbor's prime farmland over something as trivial as a conscience.

And as Socrates probably said, "Nothing illustrates our superiority over the animal kingdom like blind, indiscriminate violence."

But being the office gossip is not only a good way to get yourself fired – it's also a good way to get _other people_ fired. You remember Larry Craig, the Idaho senator I mentioned in _Fake Your Resume_? Well, he decided not to run for re-election – i.e. fired himself before other people could – primarily based on the allegation by a single Minneapolis police officer that

Craig had solicited him in an airport restroom. Perhaps the accusation is true, and perhaps it isn't – we'll never know. But what we *do* know is that the very act of making such an accusation led directly to the end of Craig's political career.

So although I've spent most of this chapter telling you how to use gossip as a force for evil, it can also be a force for good. You know you're on your way out – you've made the right decision. But a lot of your coworkers have not. They've been brainwashed by the employed masses, and they're too weak to free themselves from their prison. They're trapped in the Matrix[4], Neo, and it is up to you to release them. So the next time your company goes through a round of layoffs, remember to throw in a few words about all the people around you. If you're leaving for the sweet freedom of obsolescence, the least you can do is bring a few others along. Trust me, they'll thank you eventually.

Gossip About Yourself!

You must think I'm crazy. "Get off the peyote, Reverend Havens[5]," you're surely thinking, "who on *Earth* would gossip about them*selves*?" Given the generally unflattering nature of gossip, it would surely be folly for anyone to share deprecatory information about oneself.

---

[4] Ah, *The Matrix*. Never have I seen a movie trilogy start so well and end so badly. I mean *Indiana Jones and the Kingdom of the Crystal Skull* sucked a big one, but *The Matrix Revolutions*? If you own that DVD, be sure to hide it behind your DVD box set of *Saved by the Bell* – it'll be less embarrassing.

[5] I feel like I deserve an additional honorific, so I'm giving myself one. Plus, I really am a reverend, thanks to the twin glories of the Universal Life Church and the Internet. Seriously, I've got the credentials to prove it. I freaking love the Internet.

And yet tons of people do it! Self-gossip – or as it is more commonly known, bringing personal problems to work – is a very popular strategy to make you into the last person anyone wants to sit with at lunch. The more you complain about your broken relationships and unfulfilled dreams, the more your coworkers will breathe a collective sigh of relief when your boss finally decides he or she can't take it anymore.

Self-gossip generally falls into one of two categories: talking about fixable problems and then ignoring every solution that anyone offers; and talking about problems no one can do anything about. In either case, do *not* bother to wait for somebody to ask how you're doing before you tell them. Stop people in the hallway and launch into an extended diatribe about your landlord and his repeated eviction notices; close the breakroom door and regale whoever's trapped inside with details of your sister's fourth pregnancy with her third live-in boyfriend; interrupt a conference call to mention that your car just got repossessed; inject some fun into your business emails by talking about your father's recent arrest. And don't forget medical issues! Talking about your various ailments can be a great way to turn yourself into the office pariah. Common choices include:

- Rashes!
- Hair loss!
- Particularly noxious gas!
- Neck cramps and other minor complaints!
- Phlegm![6]

---

[6] Which is also the dumbest looking word in English. If all English words were spelled like this one, then my full name, Jeffrey, would be spelled Geophphreigh. All hail Geophphreigh!

- Psychological issues!
- STDs!
- Menopause![7]

To make yourself truly insufferable, make all your conversations as one-sided as possible. To that effect, don't *ever* ask anyone else how they're doing unless you can be certain they will give you a brief answer that will allow you to launch into your own exhaustive litany of woes. In no time at all you'll be able to watch your coworkers stop in mid-stride and turn the other direction whenever they see you coming – the perfect time to catch up with them to share the news about your gouty ankles!

"But Reverend," you might be thinking, "what if I don't have any problems to share?"

Please. You're insulting me, and you're embarrassing yourself.

The best gossips never stop talking. They start the moment they walk in the door and don't stop until they're halfway to their car. And if you do this right, your coworkers won't be able to get you out of their heads until they're crawling into bed for the night – and some of them won't even be able to stop there. They'll twitch and shiver under the covers as you dominate their dreams, nightmares that only end with their hands closing slowly around your imaginary neck.

Well, I think you now know how to use gossip to get fired. The only problem with this approach, as with using the

---

[7] *Especially* if you're in your mid-twenties.

Internet, is that it's a slow burn. Rumors have a tendency to take on a life of their own,[8] and it can take months for your coworkers to realize that you are at the nexus of them all. But don't worry. Eventually they'll catch on, and once that happens you will be universally hated and mistrusted, exactly the kind of relationship you need to forge with your coworkers if you want that coveted pink slip.

But there are more ways to alienate your coworkers than by actively working against them. Gossip and intolerance are great, but sometimes you can inflict just as much damage without interfering with anybody else's life at all. The following chapter will show you how to annoy people just by sitting at your desk and talking to yourself – which I do all the time, by the way, and is the reason why I have no friends.

But enough about me.

---

[8] Remember that telephone game you played in elementary school where you'd sit in a line and whisper a sentence to the person next to you, and she'd do it to the person next to her, and so on until the end. And five or six permutations later the original, "My house is at the end of the street" got turned into "My horse is acting like a parakeet"? Well, rumors work like that, except they tend to make even bigger jumps. For example, it only takes three generations for "So-and-so took an extra vacation day this week" to turn into "So-and-so contracted gonorrhea from someone they met at a bus station and is covered in boils." It's true – I made that rumor happen once. Got me fired pretty quick, too, since it was about my boss. I'm telling you, people, I know how to lose a job.

Whining, Grumbling, Petty Complaints – And Don't Forget Groupwork!

Oh, my, *God* – I am so *sick* of writing this stupid book. Do you have any idea how many better things I could be doing? Here I am, wasting my youth in front of this stupid computer when I could be seeing the world or saving the rain forests or driving my race car. Oh wait, that's right, I don't *have* a race car, because I don't have any time for one, because all I do is sit in front of this computer all day and wait for death to take me. And don't even get me *started* on money, because they are *not* paying me enough to sacrifice my healthiest years on this crap. *Gawd* I hate my life. Why don't I quit? Because I can't afford to, that's why, and thanks very much for reminding me. Don't you think I'd quit if I could? And to make things worse, I have to deal with *people* all day, editors and designers who are all like, "I don't think we should use the Franklin Gothic font for the Ennui sections." Uh, excuse me, did I ask for anyone's opinion? No I didn't, because I don't want it, so keep your stupid little thoughts to yourself. I don't need anybody intruding on my life any more than absolutely necessary. Because I've scanned through my contract, and I don't remember seeing 'Be Nice To Annoying People' in my job description, thank you very much.[1]

The bitter, disgruntled person depicted above has been brought to you courtesy of countless workers across America, whose uncooperative and belligerent attitudes have been helping them get fired for as long as there have been places to get fired from. Constant complaining can often serve as the last straw for employers who are already suffering from your incompetence and nonexistent work ethic, and it is a technique you should add to your lunchbox.

As you can see from the title, this is something of a catch-all chapter. However, while the advice you're about to receive might seem to cover unrelated subjects – and indeed, you'll see connections to several of the chapters you've already read – the truth is that everything in this chapter stems from the same source: namely, from *within* you. A world-class whiner is born, not made. And just in case you're dumb enough to believe that you don't have any whiner in you, all I ask for is two minutes. If I haven't convinced you in the next 500 words that you have the necessary prerequisites to complain with the best of them, then smother me in syrup and call me a cupcake.

"It's Not Fair!"

That pretty well says it all, doesn't it? The first trick to effective complaining is believing that you have come out on

---

[1] A little insight into the mangled carnival ride that is my brain: when I first wrote, 'Oh, my, *God*' at the start of this paragraph, it was a tremendous effort to refrain from continuing with, 'Becky – look at her butt.'

the losing end of everything. This should be especially easy if you have just left college[2] for the working world.[3] The simple act of leaving the magical fairy-world of college can convince most people that real life isn't worth living, and the culture shock alone can often transform the most congenial person into a hard-core whiner by the end of their first employed month.

However, if the fact that people now expect you to do things (on a deadline and without exception, no less) isn't enough to make you rail against the injustice of it all, it won't hurt to remind yourself how good things used to be. Remember how free you felt as a child, able to run and play at will without anything more pressing than cooties to occupy your thoughts? Or how easy your high school jobs were, when people paid you to stand behind a counter doing nothing for four hours at a time? Or how great your childhood home was compared to the one-bedroom dive you're currently renting? Cloaking your past in the golden halo of memory will help make the harsh reality of your current life all the more apparent, and sooner or later you'll feel compelled to share your pent-up rage with others – which we'll get to in a minute.

But if reflecting on your idyllic past *still* isn't enough for you, the surest way to begin complaining about your lot in life is to watch five consecutive hours of television. I keep mentioning television because it is such a versatile tool. Case in point: during any five-hour block of TV, on any combination of channels, you will see the following:

---

[2] Where nobody ever tells you what to do.

[3] Where (at least at first) almost everybody tells you what to do.

- People who are more attractive than you are
- People doing more interesting things than you're doing
- People who are wealthier than you think you'll ever be
- People who are more influential than you
- People who are younger, richer, more influential, *and* doing more interesting things than you are

Television does a phenomenal job of compressing all the best moments of other people's lives into digestible blocks of time, and it does so relentlessly and with no consideration for the truth.[4] After five hours of uninterrupted viewing, I can guarantee that you'll view the entry-level purgatory of your new job with bitter disdain. After all, your college degree is supposed to have earned you straight into a six-figure salary somewhere in the upper echelons of management, so why hasn't it happened already?

That was 515 words. How am I doing?

Just Passing Through

Once you've acknowledged the inherent inequity of the world and your place in it, you'll want to start sharing that revelation with others. And there's no better way to showcase yours than by telling everybody that the job you currently hold is merely a stepping stone on the path to bigger and

---

[4] Honestly, from the way the commercials depict it, you'd swear that getting herpes would make your life *better*. I'd love to go surfing or kayaking or mountain climbing all the time, the way all those Valtrex people seem to.

better things. This tactic has the advantage in most cases of being absolutely true. The job you have is beneath you, it's an embarrassment to a person of your prodigious capabilities, and you should waste no time in making that opinion known to all.

There are several advantages to this line of thought. The first is that it will help you treat your current job as a menial chore unworthy of your full attention. Soon your performance will decline – *Improve Your Incompetence,* anyone? – but you won't care since the job isn't worth having in the first place. Treating your job as an unpleasant but necessary step to something better is a great way to pay lip service to the people paying you, the way ethnically homogenous schools put white, black, Asian, and Hispanic students on their brochures to pretend that they care about diversity.[5] In your case, this will annoy both your bosses and coworkers – the former for having to listen to you complain about the job they're paying you for, and the latter for having to listen to you at all.

Which leads to the second major reason you should treat your job as an obstacle rather than an opportunity – namely, that your criticism of your job as an unimportant waste of time will simultaneously serve as an implicit condemnation of everyone else who shares your job. And let's face it – that's exactly what you'll be doing. After all, *you* know that your low-level job is hardly the right place for a person of your talents and abilities, and the only way the people around you wouldn't act the same is if they're not as smart, ambitious, or competent as you. You should see shades

---

[5] Oh, the truth can be brutal, can't it?

of **Flaunt Your Intolerance** in here, but even if you don't I guarantee your coworkers will. Every one of them will see your disgust as a thinly-veiled attack on them, their tastes, and their aspirations, and they'll begin to wonder – quietly at first, then more openly – why you're working alongside them if you're so much better than they are. You'll know that all the stars have aligned when they hate you as much as you hate your job.

So, to recap: we began with a vague sense of cosmic imbalance, which led to a concrete sense of injustice, which led to private grumbling that a small number of your coworkers have been forced to overhear. But how do you turn what is so far a localized conversation into a global one?

Have You Already Forgotten Facebook and Twitter?

This solution is so good it's hard to understand how anybody ever got fired prior to the invention of the Internet. You remember **The Internet**, right? Well go back and skim through the section on blogging and social networking, because the vast world of online diary-keeping has opened up a brave new world of passive-aggressive firing possibilities – complaining about your coworkers on Facebook, Twitter, LiveJournal, LinkedIn, and any other social networking site that strikes your fancy.

Now if you've paid any attention to this book, then you should have already opened a Twitter account, which means that you are accustomed to posting every thought as it comes to you, regardless of its tactfulness. So just keep on keeping on! Anytime a boss comes down too hard on you or a coworker wears a terrible pantsuit, anytime you have a sexually indecent thought about a colleague[6] or dream about pushing somebody down the stairs – in short, any time your lust, hatred, envy, disgust, or condescension requires an outlet, just barf it all onto your computer screen and hit that beautiful 'Post' button. The catharsis alone is reward enough.

But wait, there's more! Because eventually – and this is an iron-clad promise – the people you work with *will* discover what you've written. How do I know? Repeat after me:

Nothing on the Internet ever, *ever* dies.

That's as certain as the whole death-and-taxes thing. Everything you ever do online remains online forever, nothing ever really gets deleted, and all you need is a little time for people to find what you've done – especially when you've made absolutely no attempt to hide it.

"But of course I've made efforts to hide my indecent posts from prying eyes," you might be thinking. "I'm not an idiot, I know better than to let everybody read everything."

Ha, I say. And again, *ha*. Maybe you think you've covered all your bases, but think again. One of the beautiful things about social networking sites is the impossibility of having a closed network. Facebook, for example, pretends to limit your friends to people of your own choosing, but we all know it's a simple matter to look at the posts and pictures of people we've never met.[7] And there are now entire websites

---

[6] We'll talk more about this in **When All Else Fails, Sexual Harassment**. Don't worry, people – it's coming.

[7] And if you didn't know, you know now. Thanks to the fact that Facebook lets you look at the tagged pictures of your friend's friends and that whole six-degrees-of-separation thing, ten minutes on Facebook can get you into the White House. Enjoy.

devoted to ranking the most egregious Twitter offenses by date and topic. So say whatever comes to mind! It's fun to complain in private, but it's even *more* fun when those supposedly secret complaints rear their carbuncled heads.

Now there's a decent chance the job you've just acquired was recently vacated by a person who got fired for posting vulgar, racist, or otherwise inappropriate comments online. If that happens, most of your coworkers will tell you about it, calling it one of the stupidest things an employee could do. But those people aren't looking to lose their jobs. So who's the *truly* stupid one, huh?

"You Want Me To Do *What*?"

It's time to move from under-your-breath muttering (and the pseudo under-your-breath muttering of Internet postings) and into full-throated complaining. At some point, your contempt for everything and everyone around you will require an immediate outlet that the impersonal Internet simply cannot provide. When that happens, the best kind of complaining will be outright refusal to do whatever you're asked to do. We talked about following directions in *The Not-Quite-Eight Habits of Highly Defective People*; now we're going to talk about how to ignore them. It'll be easy – so easy, in fact, that as long as your swivel-chair can do a 360,[8] you

---

[8] Completely random side note: I had a friend once who quit drinking and told everyone by saying, "I'm turning my life around, guys, I'm doing a complete 360." Not a 180, which would point him in the opposite direction, but a 360, which would end him up exactly where he started. But I guess he knew what he was talking about, because three days later he was arrested naked on a construction crane because a bottle of tequila told him he could fly. He's dead now.

should be able to do everything in this section without leaving your desk.

The first thing to do is adopt a perpetually irritated expression – put out, put upon, the kind of face that says, "I hate my life and everybody who comes into it." This is a lot easier than it might sound, at least if you were ever an American high school student. The American teenager is unquestionably the whiniest creature on the planet, and I know you were no exception.

Hallmarks of the Annoying – Self-Quiz

* Responding to a parental request by saying, "Moooom!' with at least four o's.
* Reacting to somebody else's comment with that silent cough-snort thing people do that always makes me want to punch them in the face. You know what I'm talking about.
* Following that cough-snort thing up with "*Gawd*" and then stomping one or both of your feet.
* Turning the words "I don't want to" into a single, drawling syllable of petulance – "Iowanna!" – which looks like four syllables unless you do it right.
* Answering any comment with "Whatever," especially if you extend this from its normal three syllables to four: "What-(pause)-*ev*-er!"

Did you score 5 of 5? If so, congratulations, and I'm sure I'd hate you if we ever met. But even if you're only guilty of one of the above offenses, you still have within you the seeds of the brazen, gregarious whiner I'm going to help you become.

After you've returned to your teenage roots, the rest should come naturally. But don't take my word for it. Let me show you the power you now have in your grasp:

Scenarios to Suckle On

Boss:	"Do you think you can get the books cleaned up by Friday?
You:	"Uh, yeah, Iowanna."
Boss:	"Hey, we've got a conference coming up next month, and I'd like you to go with me."
You:	"(Cough-snort.) *Gawd*."
Coworker:	"Can you help me on this layout? I am totally stuck."
You:	"What-(pause)-*ev*-er."

Feel free to conjure up your younger self anytime anybody asks you to do anything. However, you won't have many occasions to say 'Moooom!' or 'What-(pause)-*ev*-er' without sounding crazy, which might get you a trip to a work-sponsored psychologist but will *not* get you fired. So to better fit your adolescent whininess into the milieu of the corporate world, there are a couple additional sentences you should master: "It's not my job," and "They're not paying me enough to do this." These are favorites in every working environment, and you would do well to mimic the legions of sour, discontented people who have come before you and evolved these two jewels of antagonism.

Doorway to Ennui #2 –

"It's Not My Job" and "They're Not Paying Me Enough to Do This."

At several times in your professional life, you are going to be asked to do things entirely unrelated to the reason you've been hired. Some will be minor (filling the copier, picking up a client at the airport, bringing bagels and coffee for everyone at the Monday morning meeting), and some will be more involved (taking over partial duties for a coworker on maternity leave, staying late to beat a deadline). But in either case, one of these two powerful sentences will put you on the road to the unemployed, impoverished existence you so desperately seek.

The first of them – "It's not my job" – is simply designed to get you out of doing something. There's a lot to recommend it. For one, it implies that you've read your contract to the letter and know exactly what you are and aren't obliged to do, a laughably absurd claim to make from somebody who probably signed up for a credit card and cell phone service plan without reading the fine print of either contract. Third,[9] "It's not my job" indicates a rigid adherence to detail that should by now be in direct contrast to the shoddy work you've been doing. It also displays your absolute lack of interest in helping anybody else with any unexpected problem that might come up, a good trait to develop in preparation for the section on groupwork that we'll be getting to shortly. And last but hardly least, "It's not my

---

[9] I know I skipped the second one. I had a second point in there, but I didn't think it was very good, so I just cut it out and went straight to my third point.

job" is a *really* annoying thing to say, one that's sure to grate on your colleagues like rusty nails scraped across a chalkboard.

However, when your attempts to avoid working have failed, you can always turn to the other doorway to ennui, "They're not paying me enough to do this." This sentence performs the double function of demanding a raise while refusing to the do the extra work that might lead to one – frickin' genius, I tell you! Is there any amount they *could* pay you that would make you assume extra duties without complaint?   Not a chance, my pouty-lipped friend, and everyone knows it. "They're not paying me enough to do this" is the ultimate in irritation, because while it masquerades as a sentence one might mutter to oneself, it is *always* spoken within earshot of others.

As should be perfectly clear by now, you should never make any attempt to go beyond your job description in any way, and nothing says whiny, self-centered, uncooperative beeyotch[10] quite like these two sentences. Remember them, use them, and watch the magic happen.

Such public displays of disaffection will go a long way toward encouraging your coworkers to write you off as a venomous ball of unhappiness. But there's one more thing we absolutely have to cover if you hope to fully capitalize on the acerbic personality you've worked so hard to create.

---

[10] It's not a curse word if it's misspelled. I refer any dissenters to *frick, shoot,* and *darnit* as proof.

Groupwork – So Important
It Deserves Larger Type!

We haven't spent a great deal of time discussing your interaction with others on a business level. Yes, I've shown you how to make others hate you for who you are and how you interact with them, but I haven't really shown you how to make them hate you for how you *work* with them. Do you remember a few chapters ago when I said that elementary school is when you first learned to despise other people? Well it's true, and the reason it's true is because that just so happened to be your first exposure to the hatefest that is groupwork. So pay close attention, OK? Because although this is only a single section in a single chapter of this book, it is one of the most important ones – the kernel, if you will, in the steaming turd that is your professional self.

Step One:
State Loudly and Often
Your Preference for Working Alone

This is the first step in making yourself a thoroughly detestable member of your group. The American workplace is a team-oriented environment, and nothing can aggravate those around you quite like telling them that their existence is an intrusion upon your otherwise enjoyable day.

Now you can talk all you want about how little you want to work with other people, but it won't matter – you will almost certainly be assigned to a team. However, setting the tone up front will be important for everything that follows. You want to establish yourself as uncooperative and antagonistic, the kind of belligerent maverick[11] that promises to make every project twice as long and half as good.

And how do you deliver on that promise? I'm about to tell you.

Step Two:
Avoid a Leadership Role

This should be natural for anybody with as little ambition as you have. However, there's more than just an "Iowanna!" to justify this step. Because if the project you're assigned to happens to go well – heaven forbid, but it does sometimes happen – then who do you think is likely to receive the lion's share of the credit? The workgroup leader, that's who. And it's much harder to get fired when everyone is praising you for your vision and execution.

Your only real concern here is to somehow persuade somebody else to assume the role of team leader. In many cases this will be taken care of for you, as there are often plenty of people dumb enough to want the position in order to help 'advance their career,' whatever that's supposed to mean. However, if nobody steps into the leadership vacuum, there are two courses of action open to you:

Flattery – You want to find somebody with an inflated sense of their own self-worth. This will

---

[11] *Man* I'm sick of this word.

not be difficult.[12] Once you've selected a target, engage. "You know, (whoever), we're putting a new group together and I think you should lead it. You've got the knowledge, the know-how, the people skills – frankly there's nobody I'd rather work for here than you." Because there are people, *tons* of people, who buy that kind of crap, and you need to exploit that flaw in their character.

Fear – If flattery won't work, succeed through fear. Here you'll want to center on a timid officemate, one who shakes a lot but doesn't drink coffee. If you're uncertain who to pick, drop a phone book in the breakroom and see who jumps. Then, get that person alone and say the following: "You know, (whoever), they're putting a new group together and I think you should lead it, because I've heard some things. Not about *you*, necessarily, but I think this would be the perfect chance to show the company the kind of go-getter attitude they really like around here, because I'd hate to see you go." The simple threat of an unexpected firing, especially for people ignorant enough not to have read this book, will often be enough to push someone into a leadership position they would otherwise never have sought out.

---

[12] Likely candidates include anybody who answers their cell phone in the bathroom because they think the world just can't wait, anybody with a hard-top convertible, and anybody who brags about their watch.

Once this step is complete and you've found your willing or unwilling group leader, strap on a party hat and break out the crepe paper. Because now the real fun can begin!

Step Three:
Don't Do Anything!

This should be so obvious that I'm embarrassed to write it. By this stage in your life you've been assigned to dozens of groups – in grade school, high school, college, intramurals, sports teams and the occasional game of strip poker – and you're undoubtedly familiar with the secret to all groupwork: that every project will get done whether or not you help. Your project leader will feel obliged to see the whole thing through, and the rest of your group won't want to suffer from your inaction and will generally pick up your slack.[13]

---

[13] Presuming, once again, that they haven't read this book. There's no telling how this will all shake out once this is the most popular book in the world. I suppose I'll have to re-write this section – or better yet, I might just write a sequel called *Told You, Didn't I?* It'll be a short book, since by then everybody will be out of work and won't have any money to spend on reading, but I'll need to write it in order to fulfill my master plan, which is:

1) Write *How to Get Fired!* and make it into the most popular book in the world
2) Write sequel to *How to Get Fired!* and make *it* into the even more most popular book in the world
3) Use my wealth and prestige to gain an influential position at NASA
4) Lead expedition to colonize the Moon
5) Once Moon becomes self-sufficient, encourage Moon to secede from Earth
6) Become first King of Moonlandia

So the best thing for you to do is lay low and keep applying the skills you've learned thus far. The fact that you are now in a group should serve as further inducement to be as lazy and unproductive as possible, since it will be far more likely that others will notice your utter lack of effort.

Mmm, lack of effort...

Mmm...

...

...

...

Step Four:
Delegate Everything!

In order to facilitate your ability to screw off instead of doing your part of a group project, you'll want to master the art of delegation. In practice, this tends to be the job of the project leader, who parcels out assignments to each group member in much the same way a computer routs different functions through different processors in an effort to maximize efficiency. Which is why it'll be all the more special when *you*, as the lowly do-nothing peon that you are, start telling everyone else what they should be doing!

To get the most mileage out of this, start with minor delegations – asking a colleague to compose a particular email, for example. You'll have to begin this *before* you've established yourself as a worthless member of your team; if you don't, nobody will listen to you. But people being the gullible dupes that they are (see *Gossip 101* for a refresher if necessary), most of them will happily accede to your initial requests with the blithe assumption that you have something more pressing to attend to.

Then, just as with gossip, you'll want to slowly ramp it up. It's difficult to give specifics when there's no telling what kind of project you'll be working on, but basically you'll want to source every major component of your project – research, intra-office communication, editing, design, testing, market analysis, etc. – to other members of your team. This can most effectively be accomplished through a blizzard of phone calls and emails, a technique that employees the world over have used to make others think that they're actually working. An example follows:

Feel Free to Steal This Sample Email – It's Priceless

Hey, (name), I'm totally swamped today, and we need the specs for the (whatever you need the specs for) ASAP. Can you get those for me? Thanks!

Note the 'Thanks!' at the end, which functions to turn your question into an ever-so-subtle demand for compliance; after all, who can say no after you've gone to the trouble of thanking them for agreeing to do it? Oh, and did you notice the lack of explanation as to why you're 'totally swamped' today? Which person on your team is going to be rude enough to insist upon the details of your overwhelming workload? None, that's who! N-O-N-E! MWAH HA HA HA HA!

This email is a true gem, and a few of these every day will ensure that you won't be responsible for anything. If you have no choice but to use the phone as your tool of delegation, make sure you're certain that the person you're calling won't pick up. As long as you never give anybody a chance to question you directly, you should be fine.

Now I realize some of you might look at this and think, "Boy, delegating responsibility sure sounds like a lot of work, and aren't I trying to get out of doing work?" Yes you are. But that's the beautiful thing about this – it *looks* like a lot of work, but it *isn't*. Sure, you might spend an hour every day composing dictatorial emails and phone messages for everyone on your team, but that's not much compared to the eight or ten hours you're supposed to be working. Plus, once you do this for a while you'll realize that manipulating others through incessant delegation is a joy, not a chore. It won't feel like work at all, and soon you'll come to crave it the same way you should be craving that John Belushi-sized speedball you've been working your way up to.

Eventually, though, your teammates will begin to suspect that they're doing more than their fair share of work, and one of them will work up enough courage to confront you. And this is where you'll get to pull out your most insidious weapon – the argument that delegation *is* your job! Haven't they seen all the emails and phone calls you've been sending? You've been running yourself ragged trying to keep everybody on task and keep this project on the right timeline, and now somebody has the audacity to question your commitment? The *nerve* of some people!

Enjoy, little worker bee. It's an exciting world you're about to enter, and I hope you make the most of it.

Step Five:
Outsource Blame!

If you've been even halfway successful up to this point, your project will almost certainly fail, and one of your superiors will eventually come around to ask whose fault it is. When that happens, you'll want to immediately assign the blame to anybody but you.

Outsourcing blame is a time-honored tradition among the pantheon of despised employees, and it's one you should ascribe to as well. And to help you remember this all-important step, I have a rhyme for you.

Don't linger – point the finger

That's right, folks – blame early, and blame often. Let everybody on your team know that none of them are doing a decent job, and that you are the only one doing any real work. *Then* – and this is my favorite part – let them all know how much better things would be if you'd been put in charge. The irony here will be so overwhelming that those around you will be rendered mute as they attempt to understand how so many contradictions can be squeezed into such a tiny brain.

Now as with several pieces of advice in this book, this one might seem counter-intuitive. After all, if you're looking to get fired, why wouldn't you want to *accept* the blame for a project's failure? Wouldn't that be a faster, more reliable route to sweet, sweet unemployment?

Strangely enough, the answer is no. It *might* get you fired, if the project was important enough that its failure can't be tolerated. But in many cases your boss will not only forgive you a handful of failures but will actually *appreciate* your honesty in admitting that you let your teammates down. The mark of a true leader – which of course we want to avoid – is somebody who can accept responsibility for his or her actions, both the ones deserving of praise and of rebuke. If you indicate that you recognize your failings, your bosses might assume that you've *learned* from them and will be that much better next time around.

However, if you blame somebody else, especially somebody undeserving of that blame, two things will happen. One, you'll get caught. Unless there are only two people on your team, the rest of your group will know whose fault it really is and will be only too eager to set the record straight. And once everyone else's fingers start pointing at you, your boss will realize that you're not only useless but also a liar. The fact that you tried to blame somebody else for your weakness will confirm that you're not interested in improving yourself, and that blessed pink slip should be waiting on your desk by the time you've finished throwing away what's left of your dignity.

Step Six:
Take Undue Credit!

This is a last resort and should only be applied if, by some miracle, the project you're "working" on actually succeeds. I know, I know – perish the thought. But occasionally your best efforts are simply not enough to overcome the talent and dedication that your teammates poured into their shared burden, and your only recourse at that point will be to hog as much of the credit as you possibly can. Let everyone know that you were the brains behind the whole thing – the puppeteer, if you will, pulling the strings of the marionettes you call coworkers – and that the entire thing would have ended in disaster if it hadn't been for you. It's going to take a bit of work to say this with a straight face, so you might want to practice in a mirror first. I promise your effort will not be wasted, even though this will probably not get you fired immediately.

So what's the advantage? Simple – the second you take credit for something you didn't do, everyone on your team will instantly hate you, deeply and forever. I'm not talking about the "I hate rhubarb" kind of hate; I'm talking about the kind of hate that will make your coworkers dream about stabbing you in the face. They spent hours slaving away on that project, and for you to come in and steal their moment of glory...well, let's just say that the simple act of taking undue credit is the best way to guarantee that everyone on your former team will work as hard as they can, without pay, to help you get fired.

And if you want to take this one to the next level – if you want everyone in your *company* to lobby for your early retirement – then you should take credit for projects you had absolutely nothing to do with. If you went to grad school you should recognize this as a favorite tactic among your professors, who often did little to help with your dissertation but were adamant about having their names attached to your paper – and in many cases, they put their names first!

"Oh no they di-in't!"

Oh yes they did!

There you have it, my friend. Following this advice is the best way to get yourself burned in effigy short of being elected a world leader, and let's face it – you don't have the drive to get your name on a ballot, much less win an election.

But there's one more area to cover. We have not yet plumbed the depths of your true inner ugliness. The final chapter in this section is the lowest of the low, the absolute gutter of workplace etiquette, and I promise you're going to love it.

So turn the page, my future office pariah! Depravity awaits!

When All Else Fails, Sexual Harassment

At long last, we have come to the pinnacle of alienating your coworkers, the apex of odium – sexual harassment.

Sexual harassment has existed from the moment that amoeba evolved the ability to reproduce sexually. But until 1964 there was no law – and thus no real negative stigma – against the practice. In the glory days of the 1950s, smacking your office partner on the bottom and miming the act of vigorous oral sex were all considered part of 'doing business,' and the job of secretary was a lot more involved than it is today. But thanks to Title VII of the 1964 Civil Rights Act[1], sexual harassment is now a great way to get yourself released from servitude faster than you can say, "Nice rack!"

How many people have been fired for sexual harassment? That's a hard question to answer. But I can say with confidence that a whole lot of people are at least trying. A 1980 survey of federal employees found that 42% of women and 15% of men had experienced some form of work-related

---

[1] Which wasn't actually enforced until 1976, by the way, when the first sexual harassment case went to court. It's possible that nobody harassed anybody during the intervening twelve years, but come on. We're talking the Sixties. Is there *anything* those crazy hippies didn't do?

sexual harassment; in 1987, the same survey found nearly identical results. In 2007, 12,510 sexual harassment grievances were filed with the Equal Employment Opportunity Commission – and since it's estimated that only 5 – 15% of people actually bother to file a complaint, the real number of sexual harassment incidents is likely in the hundreds of thousands every year.

Nostalgic Moment #5

Remember when you used to smack people on the butt as you passed them in your high school hallways? Remember when you grabbed random private parts while you were halfway drunk at a college party? Remember when you flashed passing cars on that road trip to Mardi Gras?
Yeah, that's all illegal now. Enjoy adulthood!

Many companies have entire conferences devoted to the issue of sexual harassment. New employees often have to sit through hours of lectures about the nuances of sexual harassment – what is acceptable, what's borderline, what definitely isn't – which I think is completely ridiculous since there's really only one rule to follow:

If you have to ask if it's OK, the answer is *NO*.

I once had to suffer through one of these seminars, such a colossal waste of time that I actually found myself counting the pores on the back of my hand – which just so you know is not how I normally spend my free time. What made it worse is that the whole thing should have taken five minutes, except every couple minutes some moron raised his hand to ask about a hypothetical scenario. I tell you, getting fired from that job[2] was a blessing.

Fun Re-Enactment of
One of the Longest Days of My Life

Idiot One: "What if my hands don't actually…"
Instructor: "No."

Idiot Two, four minutes later: "But suppose I'm just
trying to give someone a compliment, and I…"
Instructor: "No."

Idiot Three, on the heels of Idiot Two: "Let's just say, for
argument's sake, that I barely grazed…"
Instructor: "For the last time, people, the answer is no."

It's not that complicated. If even a tiny portion of your minute little brain wonders if a given action will be acceptable, you're not supposed to do it. Unless you've had a 100% success rate throughout your entire life where your unsolicited groping has turned into a passionate love moment, companies generally want you to keep your hands in your own pants – although if you take me too literally there, that can get you fired, too.

---

[2] Some on-the-job stocktrading, a few lengthy desk naps, not to mention that I don't know the first thing about particle physics despite my resume's insistence otherwise, and I was out of there before my second paycheck.

Sexual Harassment in a Nutshell

NO, and NO

Perfectly Fine[3]

Now I'm sure most of you, given the general tenor of this book, expect me to encourage you to sexually harass your coworkers. And I'd like to, since it's a great way to get fired.

But as much as I'd love to, I simply can't recommend it, for one very important reason. Sexual harassment is not only a great way to get fired; it's also illegal. You can get fined for it; in 2005 the average judgment in a sexual harassment lawsuit was $1.8 million, and the average out-of-court settlement was $300,000. You can also be brought up on criminal assault charges if you're too aggressive. And I didn't write this book to help you go to prison – all I want is to save you from a lifetime of productivity. You know another great way to get fired? Take an AK-47 into the office and shoot the

---

[3] Just kidding.

place up, maybe send an envelope filled with anthrax to your boss's house. But I'm not going to recommend either of those.[4]

So no, don't fondle your coworkers. Don't talk about anyone's boobs. Don't tell anyone how much you want to bone them, or whatever the female equivalent of that word is.[5]

So How Can You Get Fired?

I'll tell you. To be honest, I've been dying to tell you for the entire book. I'm so excited right now that I can hardly contain myself. Because the idea I'm about to share with you is so freaking awesome it still cracks me up. I'm serious, if you didn't bother getting to this section of the book, I am really sorry for you. You are missing out on the best idea since sliced bread.[6] I've used this next technique to get fired from four different jobs, and it's always been one of my favorites.

---

[4] However, if you want to screw your bosses over, sexual harassment might be the path for you. Yes, your victim can file a civil suit and fine you into a lifetime of hardscrabble poverty, or they can file a criminal one and send you to prison. But the actual law puts the blame on the *employer*. That's right, folks – if you harass somebody, your employer can be fined as well. So if you want to cost your employer hundreds of thousands of dollars, harass away! Of course they'll probably sue you along with the person you harassed, but who cares? You're broke, unemployed, and on your way to jail. They can't possibly take anything more from you – so you win!

[5] Ride? Mound? Jiggle? Seriously, girls, help me out here.

[6] While we're on it, what makes sliced bread such a great thing? Bread is great, and knives are great, but cutting bread with a knife doesn't seem that amazing an idea. Were ancient peoples staring at their uncut bread, knife in hand, wondering how they could possibly get all that bread into their stomachs in an orderly fashion? Greatest thing since sliced bread – how about greatest thing since bottled water? That makes sense to me, because whoever thought to charge people for something they were used to getting for free is a genius.

So here's the deal. There's a loophole in sexual harassment law that you'll want to exploit. Because as you know, it's illegal and unethical to tell a coworker that you find them sexually arousing. However...wait for it...wait for it...

It's <u>perfectly</u> legal to let them know you do *not* find them arousing at all!

So if you want to get fired quickly, all you need to do is let your officemates know how little you want them. Need some examples? Here you go!

You're Going to Love This...

- "Hey Bob! I'd rather do the shredder."
- "My word, Susan, is it just me or are you butt ugly? Seriously, take the mask off – Halloween's not for another couple months."
- "Tim...corrective surgery, it isn't for everybody – it is for you. See you at lunch."
- "Alex, you look like a slaughterhouse. Get help."
- "Hey boss! Just wanted you to know that every time my Viagra-induced erections last longer than four hours, I think of you, and bam! Like taking air out of a tire."

Can't you just see the stunned looks on your coworkers' faces as you verbally assault them for no reason? A few of these blitzkrieg barrages and you'll be the talk of the office!

Now in order to do this really well, you'll want to add a few new terms to your vocabulary. I'm sure most of you are familiar with 'butterface,' 'blockormore,' '9-iron,' and other derisive words for another person's lack of sex appeal. And those are fine – in fact, you might want to nickname the guy in the cube next to you 'Little 9-Iron,' which he'll probably think is a comment about his golfing prowess until you let him know that it refers to the fact that he's only attractive from 100 yards away. But if you work in a large company, you will eventually run out of inelegant words to use about the physical monstrosities all around you.

That's why I've always been partial to the acronym, for three reasons. First, nobody else uses them, so taking the time to do so can help you distinguish yourself as someone who takes unwarranted rudeness to a new level. Second, the acronym allows you to say several words in the space of a few syllables, which is very helpful when you want to offend somebody as you rush past them on your way to the bathroom. And third, the acronym offers limitless possibilities, as long as you're willing to put in a little creative effort.

Most of you know the acronym, which has become standard parlance in the world of online communications. There are literally thousands of commonly used acronyms now – OMG, OMNC, LMAO,[7] G2G, GBH&K, and so on – but the problem with these is that most of them aren't easy to say. You wouldn't say, "Wow, look at the time, I've really gee-two-gee," and if you did say it you'd sound like an enormous tool.

So when you develop your own anti-sexual harassment acronyms, create ones that roll off the tongue. For

---

[7] Incidentally, I don't think you should write LMAO again unless you actually *have* laughed it off.

example, SNABEATHY. Pronounced *snuh-BEE-thee*, it stands for:

Still Needs A Bag Even At Two Hundred Yards

How's *that* for evil! Not to mention the fact that absolutely nobody knows what it means, since it's a completely original creation. So when you call somebody a snabeathy, they'll be irresistibly compelled to ask what it means – and then you can tell them! How sweet is that, to force somebody to *ask* you to insult them!

The potential here should be obvious. You can come up with millions of these, and each one of them can be tailored to a specific person in your workplace. A few more examples to help get you started are below:

Acronym Time!

- **TULAG** (TWO-lagg) – The Ugliest Person Alive, Guaranteed
- **UTATA** (oo-TAH-tah) – Uglier Than A Traffic Accident
- **IPIBANNER** (EH-pee-ban-ner) – If Perhaps I'm Blinded And…No, Not Even Then
- **POBANET** (PO-buh-net) – Plenty Of Baggage And Not Enough Teeth
- **FLAMABLAM** (FLAM-uh-blam) – Face Like A Manatee And Body Like A Moose

I certainly hope you've had as much fun reading this list as I have writing it. And just think – I've left out all the curse words! This book is designed to be suitable for all ages, so just *imagine* how much fun you'll have once you start adding in all those adult words[8] you're so familiar with! In no time at all you'll have offended everyone around you and will be thoroughly ostracized. Whatever team you're on will be quick to disown you, and at some point people will stop reading your emails altogether. And then – voila! You will have made yourself entirely worthless in every respect, not only as an employee but also as a person.

So slip on your sneakers and check your teeth, my friend, because you're about to walk the Green Mile straight to HR – and from there, to freedom!

So there we have it, people! If you can think of a way to get fired that I haven't mentioned, I'd love to hear from you. But quite frankly, I think I've done a bang-up job. You now have a comprehensive understanding of some of the most successful ways to get fired that have ever been developed. As I said at the beginning of this book, thousands of people use a combination of these techniques every year to help themselves lose work, and now you know how they did it. If you happen to run across one of them, make sure to thank them. And thank me, too, while you're at it – because at the very least, people, I think I've given you an excellent primer for what I hope will be a short and inglorious career.

And with that, I am proud and honored to pronounce you...

...(drum roll, please)...

...(more drum rolling...)

---

[8] I don't really know why we call them 'adult' words, since all of us learn them by the time we're six.

Officially Unemployable!!!!

Give yourself a hand! Congratulations, my snabeathy friend! You'll never keep a steady job for the rest of your natural life!

Dealing With Those Bastards Who Call Themselves 'Customers'

Hello, and welcome to the super-secret bonus chapter! I'm thrilled that you've made it this far, and as a reward for either your tenacity or the somnolent inertia that caused you to keep turning pages long after your will to learn had left you, I want to give you a present. This chapter is awesome! It is so good, in fact, that if I could I would have sex with it.

Why is this a 'bonus' chapter? Because the topic we'll be covering – how to handle customers, clients, and other parasites – does not neatly fall into any of the Four Pillars of Poverty. Inexplicably, none of the top ten reasons that cause people to get fired specifically involve their interaction with customers. But I can assure you from both personal and anecdotal experience, treating customers like the cancer that they are is a great way to lose a job. Plenty of people still think that 'the customer is always right' and 'customers are the reason we have a business' – notions that I'll dispel for you shortly – and because of their fallacious logic, they'll often end up firing you when they should be thanking you.

Now I'm guessing you worked in some form of customer-service job in your youth. Most high school and college jobs – waiting tables, standing behind the register at a store in the mall, wandering aimlessly through the aisles at Target with that laser scanner gun thing and pretending that you're doing something constructive – most of these jobs involve occasional contact with customers. So I'm going to assume you already know that the typical customer is stupid, lazy, oafish, foul-smelling, uncooperative, unrepentant, caustic, shrill, and completely unaware of their various unforgivable offenses. The very fact that customers exist is evidence many prominent atheists use to dispute the existence of a benevolent and loving higher power, and once you've spent enough time dealing with customers you'll start to think that maybe they're onto something.

However, for those of you who have never dealt with customers before, I've composed the follow treatise so that you'll have a better idea of who you'll soon be dealing with.

Customers:
The Scourge of Humanity

The word 'customer' is derived from the Persian word _khoostaum_, which translates roughly into 'unholy spawn of the devil camel.' Since the beginning of recorded history, customers have played a major part in almost every war, famine, and natural disaster that has afflicted any human culture. These beastly creatures have been depicted in various famous works of art. For example, Lord Voldemort, the arch-villain of the _Harry Potter_ books, was based on a pair of customers J.K. Rowling overheard complaining about the temperature of their cappuccinos at Nicolson's Café, where she wrote much of the first _Harry Potter_ book; and of course the seventh level of hell in Dante's _Inferno_ is a place of unspeakable torment where the condemned not only have their skin pulled from their bodies by hot pincers but are also forced to work endless shifts in customer service call centers.

For proof that customers are the root of all evil, consider the Black Death, a plague which swept through 14th century Europe and eventually killed approximately 30% of that continent's inhabitants. Many people have placed the blame for this plague on black rats, which carried the disease and helped it spread. But since those rats originated in Asia, they wouldn't even have gotten to Europe if it hadn't been for customers, who complained so much about wanting things that merchants sailed to Asia for various goods, accidentally brought some of the rats onto their ships, and thus allowed the Black Death to happen.

And the same is true in a thousand other instances. Native Americans wouldn't have died *en masse* from smallpox if it hadn't been for European customers and their desire for gold; Southeast Asian children wouldn't be working 16 hours a day in sweatshops if it weren't for customers' demand for cheap clothing; the glaciers wouldn't be melting if it weren't for customers' thirst for oil; the Amazon rain forests wouldn't be disappearing if it weren't for customers and their insatiable need for bananas, soybeans, and palm oil.

So the next time you see a customer, remember that he or she is to blame for all the misery that has ever befallen our species. They are murderers. They have killed before, they will kill again, and they deserve nothing but your contempt.

Now if you'll excuse me, I have to go look for a new desk chair. I might pick up a hazelnut latte on the way, too. You ever had hazelnut? I don't know where it comes from, but who cares – it's *delicious*.

As you can see, if the entire human race were a single body, the customer class would be its leprous right foot. They are abominable, repugnant, loathsome – but most importantly, *they get in your way*. All you're trying to do is mind your own business, check some sports scores, update your Facebook profile, maybe mentally undress some of the people you work with. And out of nowhere come these ridiculous customers, whining and drooling, asking questions that only a dedicated employee would know the answer to and demanding a reasonable level of service. They complain about *everything*, and before you know it you've spent your whole day trying to satisfy these perennially disgruntled imbeciles when all you really wanted to do was sneak a nap at your desk.

And where has it gotten you? Miserable, frustrated, and unable to focus on any of the ways to get fired that I've been sharing with you up to this point. You come home tired and annoyed, and when you complain to your betrothed about your dreadful day he or she doesn't seem to understand the depth of your problem. You get into an argument, which leads to other arguments, and before you know it you're thrown out of your own home, forced to sleep in your car while the person you were planning to marry packs all their things and moves out. Your mutual friends blame you for the break-up and shun you, and in despair you turn to abusive drinking. Your liver goes before you hit forty, and you spend the rest of your abbreviated life jaundiced and shivering and waiting for a replacement liver that never comes. And all because you had to deal with customers.

Make no mistake, friend. Customers are pure evil, and they need to be destroyed. This is your only real chance in the entire *How to Get Fired!* program to do something truly good.

Yes, it will get you fired, but it will also allow you to sleep peacefully at night, knowing that you've done your small part to leave the world better than you found it.

So I'm sure you're wondering: if customers really are the soulless succubae that I've made them out to be, why do so many people put up with them? Well, for one, the people who employ you and who work beside you are idiots, which you should know by now if you've absorbed anything I've told you. But more importantly, they tolerate customers because they've been lied to. You have been, too, and if you hadn't picked up this book you might have lived your entire life believing the heinous falsehoods people have been passing down from generation to generation.

So let me set you straight.

Steaming Pile of Bull Poopy #1: 'The Customer Is Always Right'

You've probably heard this garbage since you were a child, and by now you've heard it so often that you probably take it for granted. Some of your bosses will slowly drain your will to live by drilling this absurdity into your head as though it is an incontrovertible fact. But let's look at it a little closer, shall we?

First of all, notice the word "always." The customer is *always* right – are you kidding me? Nothing is *always* true. Beaches are not always pretty, South American countries are not always politically unstable, and I am not always a patient lover. And when it comes to customers, most of the time they don't have the first idea what they're talking about. If you've ever worked in a clothing store and listened to a patron contend that she is normally a size 12 when everyone on the planet can see that she's really a size 44, you'll know what I'm talking about. And if you still doubt me, go into your nearest Wal-Mart and ask the first customer you see where you could find tweezers, a thimble, and a box of matches. They won't know! They'll just look at you like you've spoken another language – and if they attempt to 'help' you by offering an answer, most of their directions will be completely wrong! See? Customers are not always right.

But more importantly, who are the people who always[1] use this sentence? CUSTOMERS! That's right – it's customers who have decided, despite all evidence to the contrary, that they have all the answers. It's a pernicious sentence they have developed to bend the rest of us to their malevolent will, and they tend to use it primarily to bleed concessions out of you when instead they should be apologizing for wasting your time by their very existence.

So the next time a customer asks you in that snide tone of theirs, "I thought the customer was always right," smile through your tightly clenched teeth and show them the following chart:

Customer Syllogism

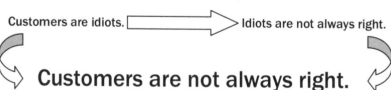

Customers are idiots. ⟹ Idiots are not always right.

Customers are not always right.

---

[1] Ignore what I said earlier about "always" not always being true. It is in this case. Don't listen to what I said before; listen to what I'm telling you now.

Yes, it would be easier to answer them with a simple "No," but most customers will be too stupid to understand what that means. The chart has pictures, though, and that'll do the trick.

Steaming Pile of Bull Poopy #2: 'Customers Are The Reason We Have A Business'

This is one your bosshole will probably hammer into your skull the second you get hired. People everywhere seem to think that without customers, all business would just magically disappear. In this fanciful version of the world customers are the driving force behind all economies, the engine of innovation, and the only reason we aren't all living in caves and sucking the marrow out of mammoth bones.

First of all, this idea is not only ridiculous but un-American. Anyone heard of Karl Marx? Well, he argued that workers were the driving force of all economies, and he ended up becoming the father of communism – which, as we all know, is a philosophy of evil. But even *he* didn't have the audacity to go one step farther and say that *customers* are the real reason business exists. He was sane enough to stay within the realm of the employed. To argue that customers are the cause of anything is to invite chaos.

But even if you support the terrorists and think that customers really are the root from which the tree of business grows, allow me to disabuse you. In order to understand the true role of the customer, you need to pay attention to money – specifically, to where all money comes from.

So, where does your paycheck come from – customers? No, of course not – it comes from your boss. And where does his or her paycheck come from? From *their* boss, whose money comes from *their* boss, and up and up until you get to the CEO and board of directors. And where does their money come from? From stockholders and investors, who get their money from their bosses, and so on and so on. Need a chart? I've got a chart.

Money Chart
(Arrow indicates where each person's money comes from)

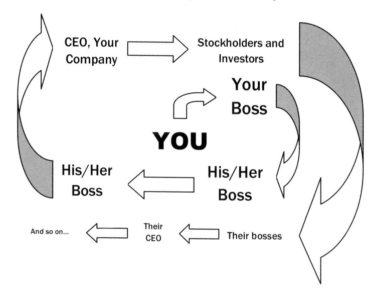

As you can see, customers are nowhere to be seen on the money chart, which means that as far as business is concerned, customers don't even really need to exist. *And*, if you'll notice, you are the center of all of this. That's right – without *you*, the whole spiral falls apart. You can't have a whirlpool without a vortex, you can't have a tornado without an eye, and as you can now see, you can't have a successful business without you.

There are two reasons I showed you this chart. The first, more fulfilling but less important, is to help you realize how incredibly awesome you are, which I can only hope will go to your head and help you with some of the techniques I've outlined in previous chapters. But the most important point, once again, is to illustrate the utter lack of importance that customers play in the whole thing. Not only are they stupid and annoying – they are also completely expendable.

"So What Do I Do?"

Easy! Treat them like the unnecessary evil that they are. Ignore them; deride them; make them wait on *you* for a change. They are not worth the breath that you will waste in conversing with them, and you need to make them aware of that as often as possible. Because only by doing so can you hope to drive them away and save your coworkers from the torment of having to deal with them.

The best way to deal with customers, as I've already hinted at, is to avoid them entirely. If you work in a store, spend your day in the back aisles or in the stockroom in an endless search for something you're not really looking for. If your customers assault you primarily through the phone, then don't pick it up! You'll get used to the incessant ringing after a while, and eventually you won't even hear it anymore – a talent that will also help you ignore you boss's orders and concentrate on that Sudoku puzzle during boisterous team meetings, by the way.

And yet customers, like zombies, never seem to truly die. They're always cropping up just when you think you're safe, and when you find yourself confronted with one, here's what you need to do:

- **Don't panic.** Customers can smell fear, and they feed on it. Take slow, deep breaths, and focus on something peaceful.
- **Display your hatred.** School your features into the tight-jawed, steely-eyed defiance you practiced so often on your parents when they tried to enforce a curfew that first summer after you'd already been away at college for a year.[2] Keep your shoulders forward and your fists clenched; you never know when a customer might pounce, and you need to be ready to take them down in case they do.
- **Say as little as possible.** Customers thrive on detailed answers to their questions, so don't encourage them. When possible, limit your answers to shrugs and grunts. Otherwise, stick to one word sentences, such as the following:
  - "Sorry, that's not my department."
  - "Let me transfer you to somebody who can help you with that."
  - "I'm actually on my lunch break, so...yeah."
  - "Well, it's supposed to be my day off, but sure, let's make this all about you."
  - "Can't you see that I'm drunk?"

---

[2] Seriously, parents, what are you thinking? They've been staying out until 3am every day for the past nine months; they're not children anymore. Besides, don't you remember how excited you were when they finally left and you could turn their bedroom into something useful? Look into your heart and ask yourself: do you really want them *around* all the time?

- **Turn away while answering.** It might seem suicidal to turn your back on a customer who could very easily attach itself to your neck like a lamprey, but it's quite effective. The average customer will be so stunned by your contempt for their power that you should have enough time to escape.
- **Walk away slowly.** Don't run! Customers move like leopards and can run down even the fastest employee. Avoid sudden movements, and do _not_ make eye contact. If a customer can see your eyes, they will follow, but they are profoundly stupid creatures. If you can't see them, they will assume they cannot see you.
- **Carry pepper spray.** It's a last resort, but it works. Be aware, though, that the cry of a customer in pain is certain to bring other customers running. You will need to leave immediately if you hope to live. Now is the time to run.

It's not a difficult regimen, and once you've done it a few times it will come as naturally to you as breathing.

The biggest danger that you'll face when dealing with customers is being converted by them. Many customers wield a hypnotic power that can turn you into one of them if you're not careful. Vampires must touch you in order for their poisonous kiss to transform you into a soulless wraith, but customers can do so _through the power of their voice alone._ The longer you talk to a customer, the more likely it is that you'll become one. A single in-depth conversation with a single customer can create in you an urge to go shopping that is very, very difficult to overcome. I don't say this to scare you but to warn you. Tread lightly, and always remember that every word out of their filthy mouths is a trap.

So now you know the truth about customers and what to do with them. I can't promise this is going to be easy. It's always difficult when you know the truth of something and can't convince everybody else that you're right. And so many of the people around you will persist in believing that customers are essential and worthy of respect that it very well might drive you crazy. If it starts to, please remember that following the super-secret bonus advice in this super-secret bonus chapter will help get you fired. While it will be maddening to listen to everyone telling you that your actions are misguided, you will at least be working toward that coveted prize of unemployment.

But the greater prize will come later, as it always must for those who follow a higher path. You did not choose to read this book; this book chose *you*. For you have been fated to call attention to a plague that walks unmolested in our midst, a sickness that has afflicted the human race from the birth of time. Many will scorn and deny you, but you must remain strong. The path you now follow is a righteous one, and when you finally ascend to the Pearly Gates or Rainbow Bridge or Gumball Mansion or whatever exotic structures are really up there, you will bask in the glory that is your due for your toiling here on Earth. You work toward more than your own unemployment, my child. You work for the salvation of mankind.

Amen.

PART FIVE:
WHAT YOU REALLY NEED TO KNOW

What You
Really Need to Know

"Wait a second, donkey boy," you might be thinking. "What's with the extra pages? I'm done with this stupid book; I've got a resume to forge, rumors to start, coworkers to harass, a fantasy league to manage, furniture porn to ogle, projects to avoid, and meth to buy. I'm swamped. Besides, I thought you already told me everything I needed to know."

Yes and no. Short of doing anything violent or illegal, you now know just about every way to get fired that there is. I left out layoffs and restructuring because they have nothing to do with an individual's performance, but I will say this: if your company is looking to lay people off, the first ones to go are the people who have done one or more of the things I've just taught you how to do.

Not only that, but I speak to over 150 business owners every year, from two- and three-person outfits to leaders of Fortune 500 companies, and when I ask them what their biggest problems with employees are, they *always* talk about one or more of the things I've just discussed with you. So in that respect, you now have all the knowledge you need to make sure you never hold a steady job – just like I promised.

But of course that isn't the point of this book. I don't actually want you to get fired; in fact, I want to *prevent* you from getting fired. I had planned to leave this paragraph out of the book since I figured it was self-evident, but my editors convinced me to keep it. So don't follow my previous advice. It's bad. Do the opposite. That's the real message, which I've now made ridiculously obvious. There – are you happy now?

All joking aside, this is definitely the most important chapter in the book, at least if you're interested to learn what every business owner in the world would tell you if they had the opportunity.

So what do you *really* need to know?

Before we get into that, I'd like you to take a look at that top ten list again.

Top Ten Reasons People Get Fired

(excluding layoffs, recessions, depressions, natural disasters, outsourcing, downsizing, or consistently failing to shower)

Lying on your resume

Unreliable work and behaviors

Inability to do assigned job tasks

Performing tasks slowly,
    with numerous errors

High absenteeism

Conducting personal business
    at work

Drug and/or alcohol abuse

Dishonesty on the job

Refusing to follow
    directions and orders

Inability to get along with others

I don't know if you noticed, but there's a lot of overlap in this list. Conducting personal business at work can often lead to poor performance – it's hard to give it your best when you're only halfway paying attention. Faking your resume is often associated with incompetence; unfortunately, some of those job requirements that employers ask for are actually requirements, not suggestions. Skipping work, or coming in drunk or high...you get the point.

The point is, people usually don't get fired for a single reason – more often it's several, a constellation of causes. And since the items on this list are interrelated, if you can correct or avoid one of these issues, you will correct or avoid several others at the same time.

So let's knock out the serious part. If you're the kind of person who likes highlighting things, now's your chance.

You might not know this, but employers don't actually want to fire people. Even the companies that outsource some of their departments aren't looking forward to letting their current employees go. For one thing, employers are human. They want people to like them, they want to think they're doing the world a service, and they know that firing people is not the way to make either of those things happen.

But from a strictly business standpoint, employers don't want to fire people because it's expensive. Severance costs money, extending health benefits costs money, hiring and training replacement employees costs money – not to mention the everpresent risk that a fired employee will decide to sue their former employer for an unfair release, since a lot of employees would prefer to think that their firing is the result of some nonexistent discrimination rather than the very real fact of their incompetence, laziness, or uncooperativeness.

There are exceptions, of course. Some employers care nothing at all for the people who work for them, and some employees are fired for arbitrary and discriminatory reasons. But for the most part, employers want you to succeed at the job they've hired you for. To that end, many employers will keep a mediocre or even substandard employee on the payroll just to avoid the hassle of dealing with firing and its aftermath. There's an old joke in corporate circles that runs something like this:

Person 1: "What do you do?"
Person 2: "I'm the CEO of a major company."
Person 1: "Really! How many people work for you?"
Person 2: "Oh...about half."[1]

Which leads me to another truth, one I alluded to earlier: every employer knows which people they'd fire if they had to let somebody go. Just as every teacher can tell you which are their most troublesome students, every employer can tell you which employees contribute the least and cause the most friction and discord. In many cases those employees are allowed to stay because, as I've already mentioned, it's often more of a headache to fire somebody than it is to simply put up with them. But in times of stress like the 2008-2009 recession, employers don't have to think very hard to decide which people to fire first. In some cases employers actually *enjoy* the first phase of an economic decline, if only because it gives them an ironclad argument for firing their lowest performing employees.

---

[1] I didn't say it was a funny joke. I just said it was a joke.

So there you have it – employers are not going to fire you the first time you make a mistake, but they will keep track. You can think of your job security on a sliding scale, much like the way you were graded in school.

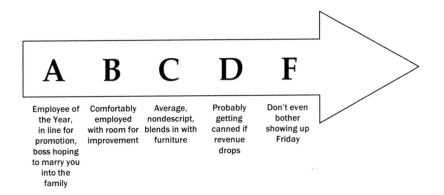

A	B	C	D	F
Employee of the Year, in line for promotion, boss hoping to marry you into the family	Comfortably employed with room for improvement	Average, nondescript, blends in with furniture	Probably getting canned if revenue drops	Don't even bother showing up Friday

You don't have to be perfect in order to be an 'A' worker; 'A' students occasionally fail or forget to turn in an assignment. And just as 'D' students get their share of diplomas, you can coast for a long time as a 'D' worker. But if you want to feel comfortable and have a reasonable hope of moving upward to bigger and better things, there are a few things you should know.

Getting a Job – To Lie or Not to Lie

So far, everything I've talked about assumes that you already have a job. But what about getting one? As of the printing of this book, the world is suffering its worst economic environment since the 1930s. In America, one person in ten is unemployed. If you're about to graduate from college, you're probably convinced that you're destined to move back into your parents' basement whether you want to or not. And for those of you who have a job but want a new or better one, you might already have despaired of ever finding anything.

Perhaps you've considered lying on your resume. It's a definite temptation, especially if you've ever been turned down for a job for lack of experience, which is the ultimate catch-22. After all, how can you get any experience if nobody wants to hire people without experience?

But perhaps more to the point, you know other people are lying on their resumes, so why shouldn't you lie on yours? It's a fairly common argument – baseball players use it to explain why they take steroids, and plenty of college students use it to justify cheating on tests and term papers.

And I'll be perfectly honest with you. If you lie on your resume, you very well may slip through, and you very well may get hired. It happens all the time, which is why so many people do it.

But there are three basic arguments against it. The first is that if you ever get caught, you will probably be fired regardless of how well you're doing. The people I mentioned in *Fake Your Resume* who got fired for lying on their resumes weren't all bad at their jobs. Some of them were – Mike Brown comes to mind. But George O'Leary was twice voted the best college football coach in the country, which is why Notre Dame hired him in the first place. However, when they learned about his forged resume, they fired him immediately. It's not good business for a company or corporation to allow employees who've lied on their resumes to keep working for them, because it will only encourage everyone else who ever applies to that company to lie on *their* resumes. Tolerating liars is generally a bad long-term business strategy.

That being said, after being fired by Notre Dame O'Leary was almost immediately hired by the Minnesota Vikings. They knew he'd lied on his resume, and they didn't care because he'd proven himself to be a very talented football coach. So if you're certain that the only thing standing between you and a successful career is a great resume *and* that you can keep anybody from discovering your misstatements for the ten or twenty years it will take to establish your reputation as a gifted employee, then go ahead and lie. Like I said, lots of people do it. But always worrying that you'll be caught and summarily fired is not necessarily the most comfortable way to face each working day.

And unfortunately for you – reason number two – it's not as easy to get away with lying as it used to be. Thanks in part to O'Leary and some other high-profile firings in the last decade, more companies are doing background checks now than ever before. In 2003, over 82% of businesses conducted background checks on at least some of their applicants, and in 2007 American businesses conducted 6,000,000 background checks on potential hires, up 20% from 2006. For some companies, background checks are standard practice. Just as the Internet has made it easier to pirate music and copy research papers, it's made it harder to slip embellishments and omissions past the people who review your resumes.

Those are two arguments against lying on your resume. But the third one is the most powerful, and here it is. If you're under 30, and especially if you're under 30 with any kind of advanced degree, the main reason you shouldn't bother lying on your resume is because you don't have to. And the reason you don't have to is because it won't be hard for you to get a job. It never has been, and until we create a society run entirely by robots who make the very notion of work obsolete, it never will be.

Actually, I'm Not Smoking Anything

Now I know plenty of people would violently disagree with what I've just said, but I'm sticking to it. It's not hard to get a job. Illegal immigrants manage to do it, and not by stealing jobs; they're doing work nobody else wants. The real problem that most unemployed people are facing right now is finding a particular kind of job in a particular location. If you have obligations that are preventing you from leaving wherever you are – family, a mortgage, whatever – then yes, it can be very hard to find a job that will support you at the level to which you have become accustomed.

But if you're fresh out of college, the picture is entirely different. For one thing, your education offers you more opportunities than most people have. Graduating from college may have been a natural step for you, but the fact is that less than one American in three has a four-year degree. If you have an associate's degree, you're still very comfortably in the top half of the country, educationally speaking. And there are several employers whose requirements include *any* college degree, regardless of the field. There's a company near my house that employs several thousand people, and they almost exclusively hire recent college graduates. They don't care what your degree is, as long as you have one, because they assume that any college graduate can learn the system they teach to their new hires. And just because you majored in a particular field doesn't mean that you'll be doing that kind of work for the rest of your life. Of the people in my graduating class that

I still keep in touch with, fewer than 25% are working in jobs related to their major. But they're all working.

But perhaps even more to the point, if you're under 30 – whether you have a college degree or not – chances are you don't have a lot of obligations tying you down. You probably don't own a home or have small children whose lives you're reluctant to disrupt by moving. Yes, you might be carrying some debt that you'll need to start repaying soon, but you can do that from anywhere. And despite everything you've heard, the job market is not universally bad. I've spoken with several business owners who've told me that 2008 and 2009 were their best years ever. Every year, in every economy, there are companies that are failing and others that are thriving. Some are laying people off, and others are hiring.

So I'll say it again. If you are not tied to a particular place, if you are flexible and willing to move to wherever the work is, you will find a job – especially if you have a college degree. If I've just described you, then getting a job is not going to be the most difficult thing you have to do.

So what *is* the most difficult thing?

Keeping a Job

The hardest thing you'll have to deal with is the fact that the job you get may not be *exactly* the job that you want. If the work is amazing, the pay might be too low; if the pay is phenomenal, the hours might be too long; if the location is ideal, your coworkers might be boring; if your coworkers are awesome, you might have to work holidays. Every job is comprised of so many variables that it's impossible to find one that will perfectly match your tastes in every respect.

But here's the really important point. Even if you *do* manage to find that perfect job, you will almost certainly have to start at the bottom and work your way up. New teachers get the most difficult classes; new police officers work the most difficult beats; new lawyers argue the least rewarding cases; new accountants handle the most mundane clients; new computer programmers write the most boring code; new airline pilots fly the most repetitive routes. *That's* the real difficulty of this leap you're about to make, and there's usually no way around it.

I've asked hundreds of business owners to describe the single biggest problem they have with their young employees, and their answers are remarkably similar. It runs something like this:

"Young people today are the laziest I've ever seen. They expect everything to be fun, and if it isn't then they don't want to do it. They come in late, they spend all day online, they expect everything to be handed to them, and they complain about having to work instead of making any effort to improve. And *then* they can't understand why they don't get promoted two weeks after they get hired. None of them wants to put any time into anything. If it can't be done in ten seconds, they don't want to do it."

And you know what? In a lot of cases, those business owners are absolutely right.

And here's why.

The Reasons

Let's see if the following description sounds like you or somebody you know.

If you're under 30 years old, chances are you were raised by hyper-attentive parents. They read 25 parenting books before you were born and tried to put everything they read into practice. They took pre-natal vitamins. They fed you preservative-free foods and lathered you in sunscreen and antibacterial soap. They made you wear helmets when you rode a bicycle with training wheels, which you couldn't fall off of even if you wanted to. They encouraged you to read early and often, and they taught you how to use a computer when you were five so you'd have a head start on everyone else. Thanks to your parents, playgrounds evolved from the tetanus-filled wood-and-metal ones that I grew up on to giant rounded plastic structures with crushed rubber matting so that even the clumsiest child would bounce right up. A lot of these changes were beneficial. There's really no good argument for children not wearing bicycle helmets, and yet almost nobody did when I was a kid. And I'm barely older than you – 31 as I'm writing this sentence.

But your parents didn't stop there. They also tried to protect you against everything that might hurt your self-esteem. To that end, they probably didn't spank you very much or discipline you in public, since either action might make you feel bad about yourself. They showered you with praise when you did well and avoided strong criticism when you did poorly. They enrolled you in sports where *everybody* got a trophy, whether or not you or your team deserved one. They let you quit your piano lessons when you got bored or frustrated. They taught you that grades could be negotiable, and some of them interceded on your behalf when you failed a test or forgot to turn in a homework assignment. In some cases, they *rewarded* you when you did poorly – a new TV for your room when you lost your first job, a weeklong vacation after a difficult semester in school – because they wanted to take the sting out of your suffering. They wanted so badly to give you an easy, happy life that they went to absurd lengths to keep you safe from every hardship.

Most of these phenomena are relatively new. I didn't get a participation ribbon or a recognition trophy when my fifth-grade basketball team finished dead last in our division, and I didn't hear any stories in high school of parents calling teachers to petition for a more favorable grade. And when I hit my brothers too hard or swore at my mother, my parents spanked me until I cried. They didn't beat me with rubber hoses or lock me in a homemade dungeon, but they definitely made sure I knew the limits to which I could push their patience.

But here's the central point. Your parents made you feel loved, safe, and taken care of. And in a lot of cases, it was the worst thing they could have done for you – not the fact that they protected you, but the degree to which they did so. You've learned that success is supposed to be easy and fun, that problems can be avoided when they become too difficult, and that failure can almost always be explained away. Your tolerance for adversity is extremely low in large part because your parents refused to let you suffer – and as a result, you are part of the most pampered, self-absorbed generation that has ever lived in this country. There are exceptions to that generalization, of course, but when business owners complain about their young employees, this is the essence of what they're complaining about: that today's twentysomethings aren't willing to do anything that doesn't have an immediate, gratifying payoff.

And if you're fresh out of college, this is doubly true. I wasn't lying before; college has been a horrendous preparation for the life you're about to create for yourself. You've chosen every facet of your day for the last several years – when you wake up, where you eat, who you spend time with, what classes you take – with almost no restrictions of any kind. You got Spring Break seven weeks into your spring semester – which was preceded with a four-week holiday, by the way.[2] Most of you have been more independent in college than you will ever be again, especially if you've had the luxury of deferring payment for your education. I don't say that to be depressing, I say it because it's the truth. You have gotten very used to having what you want when you want it, and in most cases you haven't had to work very hard to get it. And for most of you, your first 'real' job after you graduate, even if you go into business for yourself, is going to be the first time in your life when that does not happen. You are going to have to work, you are going to have to put in your time, and in most cases – and this may be the most important concept in this book – you're going to have to occasionally do things you don't want to do in order to get where you want to be.

But What If I Don't Wanna

Then you're in luck! There are a number of jobs you can get that will allow you to continue your college-like existence, and they're the same jobs you can get whether or

---

[2] Boy, I miss Spring Break. "Hey, guys, I know you're exhausted after almost two whole months of learning, so why don't you take off to Cancun for a few days and recharge the old batteries. Seriously, you've earned it."

not you have a college degree. You can wait tables, tend bar, brew coffee, be a stripper – there are all kinds of options. And there's a lot to recommend those jobs. You can set your own hours, show up drunk, skip work when you feel like it, sleep with random people – just like college! And yes, eventually you'll come in late once too often or shout one too many obscenities at your boss and get fired, but it doesn't matter when you're working at that level. There's always another bar to work at, or another pole to dance on. Turnover in those industries is extremely high – it's part of the lifestyle.

And if that's what you want, do it. It's your life, please be happy. There's obviously an enormous demand for strippers, and if I'd been born an even halfway decent-looking girl then I very well may have shimmied my way straight through college.[3]

But if you want a career, then you need to realize that the way college has catered itself to you is not at all what the working world is going to do. If you treat your job the way you've treated college, I can guarantee you won't last very long. So show up every day, on time every day. Do your job, stay off the Internet, don't take a four-hour lunch hour – basic stuff. It's not complicated.

Not As Different As It Seems

At this point, some of you are probably ready to throw the book away. "Man, this book sucks. If he's even halfway right I'm moving back in with my parents. At least *they* still love me and think I'm special, unlike the child abusers this guy grew up with."

---

[3] Because I can shimmy, people. I can drop it like it's hot.

So let me restate my position. You're not as ill-equipped to handle difficulty as I've made you out to be. You just need to realize that your job is going to function in exactly the same way as every other facet of your life.

Consider your relationships – your friends, boyfriends, girlfriends, fiancées, lab partners, cousins, ultimate Frisbee teammates, parents, and everyone else you interact with on a regular basis. Your life is built around a series of close relationships. Without these people, your life would be fundamentally different – hopefully worse – than it is now. You love a lot of these people, people whose deaths would shake you to your core, and you wouldn't trade them for anything.

And at the same time, you've probably wanted to murder all of them at one time or another.

It's the nature of relationships – the closer a person is to us, the greater their capacity to drive us crazy. If you have siblings then you know there are times when you'd like nothing more than to throw your brothers and sisters into a burlap sack and beat them with hammers. That's how it worked for me. My two brothers and I fought constantly. They called me unprintable names, and I told them that my mother never loved them and would have sold them if she could have found a buyer. But I loved them even while we were fighting, and today I look forward to every chance I get to see them. Yes, we fought, but we never let our arguments come between our relationship.

Maybe looking at your romantic relationships is a better example. It's hard to disown your family even if you want to, but it's easy to break up with a boyfriend or girlfriend and move on. And if you've ever been in a relationship, then

I'm sure you've had fights. It's almost impossible for two people to spend any significant amount of time together without getting into occasional arguments. And sometimes, when those fights are bad enough, you decide that the relationship isn't worth the headache and you break it off. But in other cases, you put up with the little arguments because you know that, taken as a whole, your relationship is rewarding enough that you can weather a few small storms.

And your job is going to function in exactly the same way. Applying to a job is like going on a first date – you're testing the waters, seeing what might be interesting. If they're interested in you, they'll set up an interview. If all goes well, you'll be hired, and your relationship with your company begins. So far everything's been great, because everyone has been on their best behavior. You've been careful to share only the most positive parts of yourself, and your new boss has only shown you the most appealing parts of his or her company.

But once you're hired – once you've gone from 'talking' to 'dating' – you're going to have some less-than-perfect moments. No matter how passionate you are about your job, there are going to be parts of it you won't really want to do. Fighter pilots fill out paperwork; CEOs attend boring dinners; musicians live in a bus and eat truck stop food; detectives sit for days on stakeouts that sometimes produce nothing; world leaders have millions of people who hate them; doctors work ridiculous hours; archaeologists spend summers burning their faces off in the desert. There isn't a single job on the planet that doesn't have its bad moments.

That's true even if you go into business for yourself. Being your own boss, setting your own schedule, and following your own vision are all fantastic, but running your own business means doing every job that business requires – design, marketing, accounting, cold calling, managing employees, writing contracts, etc. – and I can tell you from experience that you won't love every moment of it. But you'll have to deal with those imperfect elements if you want to keep doing whatever it is you've signed on to do, exactly as you do now in all your personal relationships.

Have I beaten this one into the ground yet? I'm not sure, so let's do another example – athletics. If you've played competitive sports you know that there are times when you absolutely hate it. Halfway through a double session in the weight room, six miles into a ten-mile training run, four hours into an eight-hour scrimmage underneath the August sun – whatever your sports story, I know you've had moments when you would rather be anywhere else. Training can be agony. And yet most of you stuck with it. You knew that if you wanted to compete, you had to do what your coaches demanded. You didn't always like it, but you accepted it.

I'm not trying to say that your job is going to suck and you'll just have to deal with it. What I *am* saying is that it won't always be fun and easy. But a lot of people seem to think that the working world is somehow different from everything else. It's not, and the sooner you understand and accept that, the happier you'll be.

Incompetence – a State of Mind

I know, in the back of your head, most of you are thinking that you'll somehow be able to bypass all the entry-level jobs and jump right into upper management. After all, you've always been told that you're way smarter than all the other morons around you, so surely you can skip a few steps, right?

Probably not. Employers don't promote people to positions of authority based on merit alone; they promote based on a combination of merit and experience.[4] And however much merit you think you have, you can't prove that to anybody until you have some experience to back it up. Since you won't have any at first, the people who hire you are going to assume that you don't know how to do anything – or more specifically, that you don't know how to do exactly what they've hired you for. Whether that assessment is fair or not doesn't matter; it's how they'll think. Your degree – high school, college, whatever – will suggest that you are able to learn, so they'll take that on faith and see if you have the drive, ambition, intelligence, and work ethic necessary to move yourself up the ladder. Unless you are related to the president or CEO of wherever you end up working, you aren't going to fall into a position of prominence. You're going to earn your way there.

For a lot of people, that's a difficult realization. Many of you have been taught that you deserve everything you want because you're you. But the world doesn't owe you anything. You're not entitled to a six-figure salary, or an expensive car, or a seaside mansion, or a Gulfstream jet. Perhaps you were born into those things, and they've all been given to you. But if you're like most of the people on the planet, then the only way you're going to acquire a life of ease, power, and wealth is to work for it. There's no way around

---

[4] In theory, at least. Sometimes they promote idiots. But that's another book entirely.

that. The world is not fair. And anytime you start complaining that some people have more advantages than you do, try to remember that by virtue of living in this country you are better off than 85% of the people on Earth. There are billions of people who would literally kill to be where you are right now – young, well-educated, and with an opportunity to make something of yourself – so don't complain too much if you have a slightly tougher climb than a few of the people around you. For all its inequity, America is still a country where hard work can allow you to rise as high as you want to go. And whether you voted for him or not, Barack Obama – son of an immigrant, raised into poverty – is a good example of that.

But perhaps a better example, for our purposes at least, is Tom Brady, starting quarterback for the New England Patriots. He played four years of unspectacular high school football and was enrolled in Michigan State's program as a seventh-string quarterback. Seriously – _seventh_. Until I learned this, I didn't know they had seven.[5] But he started college as a seventh-string quarterback, and he sat the bench for two years while he worked his way into the starting spot his junior year. The lack of playing time in his first two years was so difficult for Brady that he hired a sports psychologist to help him cope.

After graduating, Brady was drafted into the NFL by the New England Patriots in the sixth round, the 199th overall pick. For those of you who don't follow football, the 6th round is generally the part of the NFL draft where college players go to die; no sixth-round draft pick is expected to do very much. And indeed, in Brady's first season as an NFL quarterback, he

---

[5] I looked into it, and it turns out that the towel boy is sixth.

didn't. He started his professional career as a fourth-string quarterback and finished his rookie season 1 for 3, with a total of six passing yards. By the end of that first season, Brady had muscled his way into the backup role, where he may very well have stayed forever if an injury to the Patriots' starting quarterback had not given him an opportunity to prove himself.

What's my point? It's that Tom Brady is a guy who was told for at least nine years – four in high school, four in college, and at least one in the NFL – that he was not good enough to play at the professional level. And now some people consider him to be the best quarterback in the history of the game. It happened because he believed in himself, but more importantly it happened because he worked like hell to make it happen. It wasn't always easy, and I can guarantee you that it wasn't always fun – nobody hires a sports psychologist because they feel great about themselves.

And if you think that Barack Obama or Tom Brady or any successful role model in your life is somehow better than you are, think again. You've been following the same path to success that they have, whether you realize it or not, for your entire life. Everything you're good at is the product of years of effort.

How do I know that? Because when you were born you sucked at *everything*. You couldn't walk, or talk, or feed yourself, or control your bladder. You weren't very good at breathing or sleeping. You were completely worthless, and if you hadn't improved your parents probably would have gone insane. But you did get better, with some practice.

And you've been practicing ever since. You didn't always know how to play the guitar, ride a bicycle, write a paper, analyze opposing arguments, mediate a dispute, conduct a lab experiment, impress a girl, hit a golf ball, tell a decent joke, drive a car, speak a foreign language, cook a four-course meal, replace a muffler, design a mural, speak in public, write a decent poem,[6] build a website, or any of the twelve million other things that now seem natural to you. Some of the skills you now possess came to you unconsciously, which made it easy to learn because you didn't realize you were learning. But most of them are the result of conscious effort on your part. If you play a sport or an instrument, if you're a talented actor or magician, if you're a skilled mechanic or hacker, you came to that ability through a fair amount of hardship. And the success you'll find at your job – whether it's working for a corporation, non-profit, government agency, or yourself – is going to come to you in exactly the same fashion.

So if your job requires you to do things you don't know how to do, learn how to do them. Study, stay late if you need to. Your education is not finished once you have that degree in hand. Because if you don't make that effort, people will notice, just like they'll notice if you do well. And if you develop a reputation as somebody who is both incapable of doing what's necessary *and* unwilling to work to correct that, then nothing is ever going to happen for you. The people who get fired for incompetence are the ones who will not work to improve themselves, and if you follow their model then you're going to be constantly frustrated that everything isn't

---

[6] I know a lot of you wrote them in junior high and high school, and they're all awful. If you don't believe me, go back and read over those first sixth-grade poems. They're atrocities. "My love, it burns like fire/My love, it's full of deep desire..." Man, it hurts just *thinking* about it.

automatically easy for you, and you're professional life will be a succession of brief, unfulfilling jobs.

What Your Employers Owe *You*

So far I've spent a lot of time talking about your responsibilities when it comes to the working world. But now I think it's time to talk about what you should expect from the people who hire you. Of course you may end up working for yourself, and then it will be up to you to make your job worth showing up for. But otherwise it's important for you to know that your boss owes you more than just a paycheck.

Just as things have changed in the parenting world over the last generation, they've also changed in the working world. For our parents, and especially for our grandparents, work was primarily a means to an end. Whether they liked their job or not was not as important as having a job that provided enough stability and security to provide for their families.

But for you, most of the stability and security that your parents and grandparents got from their jobs are now gone. Fewer and fewer companies provide comprehensive benefits, almost none offer pensions, and absolutely none of you are counting on Social Security to be around when it's time for you to retire (and if you are, you shouldn't be). Thanks to the rampant increase in outsourcing across several industries over the past fifteen years, there is also very little reason for you to believe that your company is going to be a loyal employer for the next thirty years. Most of the financial arguments for staying with a given company for your entire career have evaporated.

Which means that the only thing left – the one thing that your grandparents and some of your parents were willing to overlook – is for your job to be personally fulfilling. As motivated as most of you are by money and the comforts and experiences it can bring you, you also want to be inspired, to feel like you're part of something important, to do something that matters in the world. You don't want to be a cog in a machine; you want a job that reflects who you are rather than what you do. Like I said before, you won't have trouble finding a job, and you can always find a job that will give you enough money to eat. But you want more than to save up for your retirement. You want *to want to go to work.*

There are some employers who don't understand this. It's new to them, it's not the way they think of work, and those people tend to be rigid and resistant to doing things any differently than they've always done them. You might run into a boss who simply can't understand how you can work while listening to music. I, on the other hand, can barely function unless there's music playing in the background, and any boss who insisted I work in silence would get much less out of me than ones who allowed me to work according to my tastes. The best employers, though – and there are plenty of them – will recognize that there is more than one way to do a job, and they'll do what they can to make your professional life as enjoyable and meaningful as they can.

It's a complicated dance that I'm talking about. You need to do what's expected of you whether you enjoy every moment or not, and your employers need to make your job fun and engaging whether they think it's important or not. And both need to happen simultaneously. There's no point in arguing over which side should start this process; if one group feels like their needs aren't being met, the whole thing will fall apart.

I'm speaking from experience here. I went to college to become a high school English teacher, a job I expected I'd have for the rest of my life and which I ended up quitting after two years. My reasons for quitting were very simple: my students, on average, would not do anything I assigned them. If I gave them six days to read a seven-page story, only about 25% of them bothered to read it. If I gave them a two-page worksheet to do *in class*, about a third didn't even take the trouble to hand it forward at the end of the period. Most of them didn't care, and most of their parents didn't either; at the first parent-teacher conference in my second year, only six of my 120 students' parents showed up. I had some wonderful students, of course, and I did everything I could think of to make my class as entertaining as possible. We wrote songs and put them to music; we re-did *Romeo & Juliet* as a gangster epic; I brought my drum set into class to help illustrate the difference between rhyming and free verse poetry; I dyed my hair pink as a reward to one student who had collected enough extra credit. But as a whole, my students would not meet me halfway, and ultimately I quit because of it. It wasn't the money, or waking up at 5 am every morning, or the tedium of grading papers that drove me out of teaching. It was the fact that my students couldn't give me what I needed from them.

If I could go back, I know how I'd begin each class. I'd take attendance, introduce myself, and then say, "All right, guys, here's the deal. Each of us has a job in this classroom. Your job is to do the assignments I give you, and mine is to make those assignments as fun as I can. I am promising right now that I'll do everything in my power to make this the best class you have all day. And if any of you has any ideas about how I could make it better without compromising my duty to teach you English, then I'm open to any suggestion. But you have to do what I ask of you. If you don't read what I assign or do any homework, I won't be able to do anything interesting with you, because everything I have planned requires that you keep up your end of the bargain. If you don't do what I ask of you, I can guarantee that you'll hate this class. You'll waste 55 minutes each day sitting in that chair thinking about nothing and bored out of your mind. But if you meet me halfway, I promise you'll have more fun. So there you go. You have my word, and I'm going to honor it. Ball's in your court now."

Some version of this conversation is played out in every relationship between any two people or organizations – Party A will expect certain things from Party B, and Party B will expect certain things from Party A. And it will happen with every job you ever have. But unfortunately, a lot of times this 'conversation' doesn't include an actual, verbal conversation. People tend to assume that everybody knows what everybody else expects, and a lot of problems can result from those assumptions.

So when you get your next job, take the initiative. As long as you've determined to hold up your end of the deal and are willing to work toward whatever goal your job requires of you, you have every right to tell your employer what *your* expectations are. For example:

"Hey (name of boss), I just wanted to thank you for hiring me and to let you know that I am going to do everything I can to meet and surpass your expectations. I'd like you to tell me exactly what's expected of me, so that I don't fall short out of ignorance. I know that I don't know how to do everything well yet, but I am going to learn, and I hope that nobody will have a problem if I ask questions and need a little coaching as I get up to speed. If I'm doing well or poorly in any respect, I'd like you to tell me, so that I'll know I'm doing a good job or so I can work on improving. I am going to be the best employee you've ever had. And in return, here are the things that will help me enjoy this job as much as possible."

Then *tell them.* You can't negotiate a higher salary or larger office right out of the gate – those things will come with time and experience – but there are plenty of things you should feel perfectly comfortable asking for. If you want to listen to music while you work, or leave early on Friday after you've finished everything you're supposed to, or decorate your office a particular way, just say so. So long as your request won't keep you or your coworkers from doing your jobs, your boss won't have any reason to deny you. Most of the time they should be impressed by your confidence and happy to give you what you're asking for, so long as you live up to your end of the bargain. And if they don't – if you've found yourself with an employer who expects everything out of you but doesn't give you anything in return – then chances are you won't be staying there very long. There are plenty of places to work, and you've got better things to do than waste your life in a job you can't stand.

That's really all there is to it. You need to realize that your job can't always be fun and easy, any more than any other aspect of your life can be, and that you're going to have to put in some time and prove yourself before you rise to the level you know you're qualified for. And your employers need to realize that you want meaning out of your job and that there's more than one way for work to get done, and that they're more responsible than ever for making work something you want to do rather than something you have to do. If both of those conditions are met, you'll be happy almost regardless of where you end up. There are a thousand jobs you could end up loving, and I'll be willing to bet that where you end your working life is nowhere near where you start it. Five years ago I had no idea that I would be where I am today, and I'd bet any amount of money that five years from now I'll be somewhere I don't anticipate. Your life will work like that, too. It's an amazing ride, as long as you're willing to put in the effort.

And we've covered just about everything. Only one area to go.

Coworkers – Since You Can't Shoot Them, You Might as Well Learn to Live With Them

There's no way around it – you're going to have coworkers. Even if you work alone creating websites, trading futures, conducting experiments or anything else, you will occasionally have to venture out of your hole and deal with the rest of the world. There is a very popular American myth about the 'self-made' individual, the daring entrepreneur who marches into the wilderness and cuts a path with no help but his or her own courage and determination. It is a lie. There isn't a single person alive who operates entirely independent of everyone else. All of us owe a significant part of whatever success we achieve to the legions of parents, friends, colleagues, investors, coaches, mentors, bartenders, priests, psychiatrists and spouses who have helped us along the way.

So managing your coworkers will be key to both enjoying and succeeding at whatever job you find yourself in. As I'm sure you already know, a decent group of people can improve even the most tedious job, and a bad group can drain all the fun out of the best job in the world. If you're lucky, you'll find a job where you click with everybody.

In all likelihood, though, you'll find yourself working alongside a lot of people you like and a few you would otherwise never choose to spend time with. Maybe they're super-religious or not religious enough, maybe they smell bad, maybe they have an annoying laugh, maybe they show up late or are always on time, maybe they're too obsessed with sports or shopping or boring TV shows – whatever the reasons, it's going to happen. And it shouldn't be a surprise. I mean seriously, you have *friends* you don't like all that much. There are people in your cell phone register you never call and whose calls you ignore when their numbers pop up on your caller ID. You have friends you only invite to group functions because they'll find out if you don't, and you don't want to hear them whine about not being invited. And those are your friends. So chances are you will work with people you won't ever invite over for dinner.

It's not hard to deal with the occasional difficult coworker – annoying, yes, but not hard. Often, as with your so-called friends, you can simply avoid them. When that doesn't work, you can usually suffer their presence for the small amount of time you have to until they go away again. That's what I do with one of my neighbors, whose disappearance from this planet wouldn't bother me in the slightest but who generally keeps to himself and so is only an infrequent nuisance.

But when you can't avoid or ignore a difficult coworker, the only option you have left is to be straight with them. You've done this with your friends, boyfriends, and girlfriends when they've crossed certain lines; at some point, you can't ignore the problem and maintain your relationship, and so you make a choice to either write that relationship off or come clean with all your problems in an attempt to find a way back to where you once were. And you might have to approach a coworker someday and lay it all out there:

"Hey (whoever). I know we aren't each other's favorite person in the world, but we need to get along if we're going to work together. So I'd like to know what I can do to make our relationship better for you, and I'd like the opportunity to tell you what I need as well. Can we give that a shot?"

It won't always work. There are a remarkable number of people who are determined to be unhappy. They look for problems, they define themselves by their confrontations, they've forgotten how to be courteous, and they very well may work right beside you. Even worse, there are some people who look at anyone else's success as an implicit indication of their own incompetence. Being straightforward with them, and letting them know that you're interested in making their working day better too, will hopefully do the trick. If it doesn't, then the best you can do is interact with them as little as possible and take comfort in the fact that your life is better than theirs.

Don't Be One of Them

That's how you deal with them. Now, I want to make sure you never *become* one of them.

For the most part, it's all obvious. Say 'please' and 'thank you.' Try to be genuinely happy for the success of others. Stay out of other people's private lives, and keep your own out of theirs. I know that Twitter and Facebook have made it popular to share your every thought with every person on the planet, but in the name of everything holy do *not* talk about your coworkers online. If you're compelled to complain about somebody or discuss your own personal tragedies, discuss them with someone you know will be sympathetic, and try to vary that person from week to week. There are a lot of people in your life who want to help you, but none of them wants to feel as though their only function is to be a sounding board for all of your emotional and interpersonal issues.

None of this is rocket science. But there's one more thing I want to talk about, and I'd like to share a story from my past that will hopefully illustrate what I'd like you to get out of this.

Just after Christmas my freshman year of college, I met the most amazing girl I'd ever met in my life. We auditioned for the same play, some of her theater friends knew some of my theater friends, and a group of us ended up back at her apartment the night after parts were posted.[7] Eventually everyone else either left or fell asleep, but she and I stayed up talking for eight hours.

It was incredible. I had never done that before, never found anybody that I could talk to for eight hours and still want to keep talking to.

---

[7] I got the role of 'town drunk,' and she was 'Peasant #2.' Seriously, that's what it said in the programs. Apparently she wasn't peasanty enough to land Peasant #1.

She was hot, too, which didn't hurt.[8]

Anyway, we started dating that evening.[9] And within ten days I was head over heels in love. I had never met anybody like her. She was beautiful, smart, she'd traveled, she spoke foreign languages, she talked about issues I'd never even considered before. It was amazing.

And she ended up being one of the worst people I have ever met in my life.

I don't even know how to describe how bad our relationship was. She was argumentative, intolerant, the most judgmental person I've ever met, and she hated everybody. Everybody, including me most of the time. My entire sophomore year of college was this black hole of time while she slowly sucked the life out of me. We were together for eighteen months, and I'm sure you're thinking, "Why on Earth did you stay with her that long?" Because I fell in love with her before I got to know her, which I hope never happens to you. Those first couple months were wonderful, and then we had more conversations, and I got to know her a little better, and I realized, "I don't really like you very much. You're a bitter, angry, spiteful, terrible person. But I'm in love with you, and love conquers all, so let's make this work." That's a

---

[8] Just a sidenote here, ladies. If a guy is willing to postpone sleep to stay up talking with you, he is into you. If you've ever said, "I just don't know, Jake and I stayed up talking until dawn but I don't know if... " Just stop right there. He wants you. I have a lot of great friends that I love hanging out with, but as soon as I get tired I will go to bed. If it's a girl that I want, though, I'll stay up for five days if I have to, and so will every other heterosexual guy on the planet. "No, what? No, I'm fine, I'm not tired, I was just...you know...so, what were you talking about, oatmeal, ponies, what? You're pretty..."

[9] Read into that what you will.

horrible position to be in, and it's why we stayed together as long as we did – until thankfully, one night, I walked in on her having sex with another guy, which was seriously the best thing that's ever happened to me, and I finally got out.

That's another story, by the way. If you want to hear that one, just ask me about it if we ever meet and I'll be happy to tell you. It's pretty entertaining.

Anyway, the reason I'm telling you this is because halfway through our disastrous relationship, everybody else in my life realized how bad things were. I am not exaggerating when I tell you that none of my friends or family liked her. None. Zero. And at the time I remember thinking, "Well you just don't know her like I do, if you could see inside her you'd realize how amazing she is."

And you know what I learned as a result of that experience? Pay attention:

If everybody you know thinks one way, and you disagree with all of them, _you are wrong._

This isn't necessarily true about ideas – plenty of scientific theories and successful businesses have come about in the face of universal opposition. But it is absolutely true about relationships. If everyone you know thinks you shouldn't marry the person you're with, then maybe they're onto something you haven't figured out yet.

And here's the point when it comes to your working life. If you ever find yourself saying that _everybody_ you work with has a problem, that _every_ one of them is a slacker-idiot, that your *entire* department or company or industry has its collective head stuck up its collective colon and that you're the only intelligent person in the bunch – if you ever get here, then chances are you're the problem. If I'm describing you, then you've somehow trained yourself to focus on other people's failings to the exclusion of their good qualities. That's what my ex-girlfriend did; she seriously hated everyone who was not exactly like her, which meant she hated 99.9% of the people she met. And if you live your life that way, I can guarantee you that two things are going to happen. You'll hate everyone – and everyone will hate you.

I'm not saying you can't have a problem with a few of your coworkers, because you probably will. I've worked with some thoroughly useless people, and you might too – employees who are just wasting time until they're old enough to retire, managers who can't tie their own shoes, CEOs who care more about their golf game than their company – but I've never worked anywhere where *everyone* is incompetent. If you'd prefer to believe that you're the only diamond in a sea full of coal, then do the world a favor – go into business for yourself, stay single, and don't have children. You are not the only decent, creative, talented person in the world. You are capable of incredible things, but so are the people around you. Remember that, and you'll be fine.

The Takeaways

So here they are, the ideas I hope that you've absorbed from this book. It's always a pain to distill thoughts into a few bullet points ("What's *Titanic* about? Oh, it's about a boat, and some people...you know, it's a boat."). But for those

SparkNotes fans among you – the ones who were given this book, never intended to read it, but flipped through looking for the summary – here you go.

Reason for Writing Book
(besides amusing myself and hopefully you)

1) *Be honest on your resume.* There is a peace of mind you can't get by lying, and you won't ever have to wonder when you'll be caught and fired.

2) *Realize that your professional life will function exactly the way your personal life does.* You won't love every minute of it, any more than you've loved every minute of your life up until now, but it has the potential to be incredible.

3) *Understand that nobody owes you anything, and that your success will be earned, not handed to you.* You are going to have to work – there's no way around that – and if your natural abilities aren't enough, work to improve them.

4) *Save your alcohol-enhanced acid trips for the weekend.* The hallucinations are more fun when you're not trying to give a presentation to venture capitalists.

5) *If you're about to graduate from college, accept the fact that college is ending and that your life is going to change in significant ways.* It's not going to be worse, just different. You can't treat your job the way college allowed you to treat your classes.

6) *Enjoy the Internet and its copious amounts of porn on your own private time, preferably in a soundproofed room.* Why? Because I don't want to hear it.

7) *Understand that you do not have all the answers, that you are not the only one who knows exactly what to do, and use that knowledge to make yourself a vital member of your team.* People tend to be decent to you when you're decent to them, and the ones who aren't will probably be fired soon anyway.

8) *Restrain the impulse to mount your co-worker on the breakroom lunch table.* Or the bathroom, or the copier, or the parking lot at lunch hour, or...

9) *Don't complain if you're expected to actually do your job, and do **not** talk about your coworkers on Facebook or Twitter.* If you hate your job and everybody around you that much, save yourself the trouble and quit. There are other jobs, and there's no reason for you to be unhappy any longer than you have to be.

10) *Realize that sometimes you have to do things you don't want to do in order to get where you want to be.* It's been true your entire life, and it will be true about every job you ever have.

The reason I bothered writing this book at all – besides the whole 'take over the Moon' thing that I mentioned earlier –

is because I desperately want you to be happy wherever you end up. If you're about to graduate from college, then you're about to do something incredible. Fully 25% of college freshman don't make it to become college sophomores. If you've passed that threshold, if you plan to graduate, you deserve to be proud of what you've accomplished. And I'd hate to see you throw away all that effort by earning your way into the unemployment line.

But whether you went to college or not, having a job allows you to create your own life. Up until now, you've spent most of your existence being taken care of by somebody else. You've followed a path of someone else's choosing because you haven't had the means to do otherwise. Hopefully you've enjoyed your world so far. But the second you leave that safety and take matters into your own hands, you'll have the opportunity to create whatever world you wish. Whether you go into business for yourself or work for somebody else, you'll command an autonomy you could only dream of in high school or college. That kind of freedom can be very frightening, and that fear causes plenty of people every year to give up on their own lives and return to the safety of their parents' homes. But it's also exhilarating. To determine the course of your own future – that's the real American Dream. And it's yours for the taking.

Enjoy.

Sources

Here's where I got all my information from for this book, so that you can check for yourself to see how much I was lying. I didn't lie very often, by the way, and when I did it should have been easy to catch. And just to answer your soon-to-be-formed question – yes, I realize that all of my sources are from the Internet, that the Internet is notoriously unreliable, and that half of these sources probably won't exist by the time you might care to look at them yourself. But what else do you want me to do? I don't remember the last time I saw an encyclopedia. I remember when they used to have encyclopedia *salesmen*, if you can believe it. They wore cloaks and rode dragons – it was incredible. I always wanted to be one. But then global warming came, and they all died out. It was pretty sad.

Anyway, pretty much everything you'll find here can be independently verified on your own on any number of other Internet sites or by talking to any business owner on the planet, so I'm not too worried about the integrity of my information. So enjoy reading all these links! This is probably the best couple pages in the whole book. Riveting, really. Knock yourself out.

Fake Your Resume

http://www.pownetwork.org/phonies/phonies26.htm
http://www.pownetwork.org/phonies/phonies99.htm
http://www.punditguy.com/liar-liar-resume-on-fire/
http://slate.msn.com/?id=2072961
http://politicalgraveyard.com/special/trouble-disgrace.html
http://www.super-solutions.com/EmployeesLies_Resumes.asp

The Not-Quite Eight Habits of Highly Defective People

http://www.caveon.com/citn/?cat=20
http://www.netlingo.com/acronyms.php

Treat Your Job Like College

http://en.wikipedia.org/wiki/Agoge
http://www.earthcalendar.net/index.php
http://www.cnn.com/2008/LIVING/worklife/06/10/lw.napping.work/index .html

The Internet

http://shavemyyeti.com/index.html
http://eightsolid.com/24-very-strange-funny-signs/
http://www.furnitureporn.com/
http://www.dumblaws.com/
http://www.wasteoftime.com/
http://www.license.shorturl.com/
http://www.quizgalaxy.com/quiz_83.html
http://www.malevole.com/mv/misc/killerquiz/
http://www.nytimes.com/2003/05/11/national/11PAPE.html
http://www.usatoday.com/news/2004-03-18-2004-03-18_kelleymain_x.htm
http://www.rythospital.com/clyven/lab.shtml
http://www.catalogs.com/info/health/how-many-spiders-does-a-person-swallow-in-their-sl.html
http://www.lhup.edu/~dsimanek/fe-scidi.htm
http://www.biblebelievers.org.au/holohoax.htm
http://whatreallyhappened.com/RANCHO/CRASH/TWA/twa.html
www.whitehouse.org
http://www.martinlutherking.org/
http://web.cocc.edu/zziegler/referenced%20articles/African_Nuclear_Pile.htm
http://web.cocc.edu/zziegler/referenced%20articles/anything_into_oil.htm
http://www.wanttoknow.info/9-11cover-up - the U.S
http://www.ufodigest.com/news/0108/changing-earth.html

Cocaine, Meth, and Other Things to Put in Your Coffee

http://www.theledger.com/article/20081005/NEWS/809300439?Title=Drinking-on-the-Job-Still-a-Problem-But-Not-As-Prevalent

http://blogs.bnet.com/teamwork/?p=653

http://www.time.com/time/magazine/article/0,9171,878870,00.html

http://www.time.com/time/magazine/article/0,9171,1075018,00.html

http://www.libraryindex.com/pages/2127/Economics-Alcohol-Tobacco-U-S-ALCOHOL-SALES-CONSUMPTION.html

http://www.usatoday.com/news/topstories/2008-02-21-2221217072_x.htm

http://en.wikipedia.org/wiki/Prohibition_in_the_United_States

http://www.straightdope.com/columns/read/2625/did-the-pilgrims-land-on-plymouth-rock-because-they-ran-out-of-beer

http://www.usatoday.com/news/nation/2007-03-15-college-drug-use_N.htm

http://www.msnbc.msn.com/id/17388276/ns/health-addictions/

http://en.wikipedia.org/wiki/List_of_drug-related_deaths

http://www.markhoustonrecovery.com/ingredients_of_crystal_meth.php

When All Else Fails, Sexual Harassment

http://www3.uakron.edu/lawrev/robert1.html

http://www.avvo.com/legal-guides/penalties-sexual-harassment

http://www.sexualharassmentsupport.org/SHworkplace.html

http://berkeley.edu/news/berkeleyan/2006/01/26_training.shtml

My father, Rex Havens, who is hilarious in his own right (visit www.rexhavens.com if you're misguided enough to doubt me) and whose various ideas and concepts provided the core for this chapter, including SNABEATHY and the legal acrobatics outlined therein.

What You Really Need To Know

http://www.usatoday.com/news/health/2006-04-24-substance-abuse_x.htm

http://en.wikipedia.org/wiki/Education_in_the_United_States#College_and_university

http://www.privacyrights.org/ar/LeslieFlint-BGChks.htm

http://en.wikipedia.org/wiki/Tom_Brady

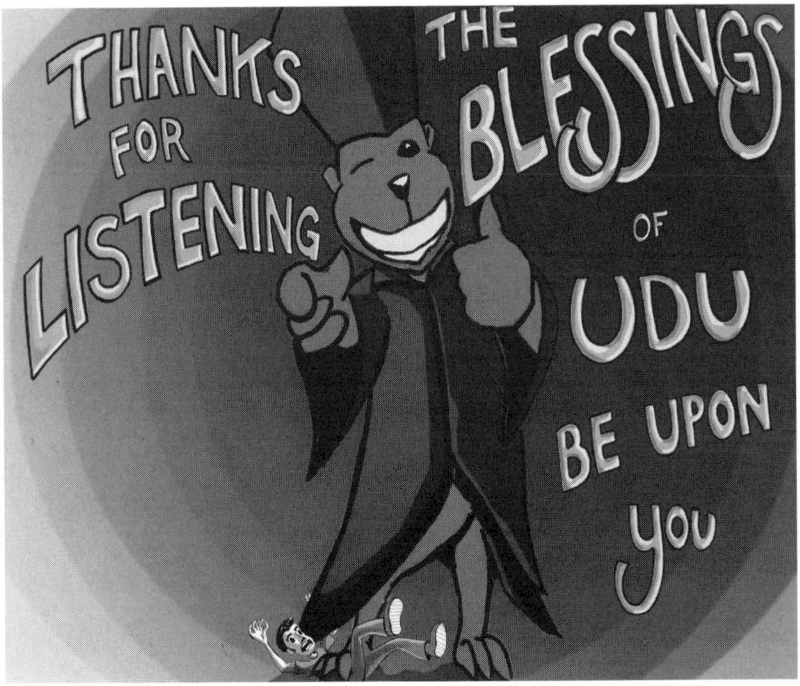
THANKS
FOR
LISTENING
THE
BLESSINGS
OF
UDU
BE UPON
YOU

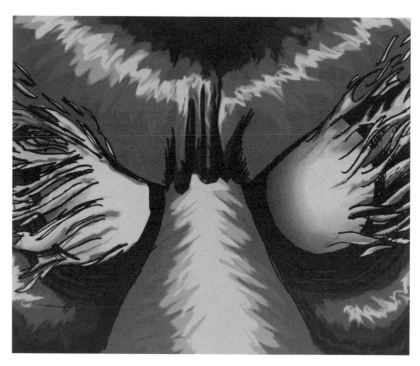

UDU IS WATCHING...